I0829578

Italian Vanguard
international edition october 2024



Translated from Italian by Alberto Brandi

Cover Art created with AI

Graphics and layout FB
Polemos editrice - Belluno, Italia
October 2024

**POLEMOS**
**editrice**

https://polemos.info/

# Adinolfi | Anselmo | Boco
## Scianca | Taietti

# ITALIAN VANGUARD

## ideas for future predators

POLEMOS
editrice

# Contents

# Preface

We are bound to abandon this distinction of different moments of time, and recognize that character is essentially non-temporal, that it exists at
the origin of all human experience and action outside of time. [...]
Character is essentially a transcendental property
that belongs to the will quite apart from any empirical relations that it may enter into in the course
of social life [...].
For if he is to have an opportunity of exhibiting
civil courage the individual must give up his isolation and enter into relations with others. Or is
there perhaps a social link between the individual
and other individuals even within the transcendental act of the will? [...]
It may be that pure will in its transcendental aspect already involves a transcendental sociality
which is the fundamental ground and source of
every society that can ever be established in the
outer world.

G. Gentile, *Genesis and Structure of Society*,
trans. by H.S. Harris, Urbana and London 1966,
pp. 94-96.

At a time when terminal capitalism seems to be hur-
tling all the contradictions of society towards an inevitable, crashing endpoint, when ancient Indo-European values are being openly denigrated and suppressed, when
the very survival of a life- and will-affirming foundation
of civilization is threatened by the deadly grasp of the
incestuous child born of late capitalism and communism,

despair and discouragement abound.

Yet this is the perfect time to ride the wave of history, just as in the epic scriptures that form the pillars of our civilization, from the Vedas to the Iliad and the Aeneid: amid the burning ashes of Troy, it is time for us to move and reclaim the land of our ancestors.

Isolation, despair and outrage are symptoms of the psycho-biological warfare waged by the negative forces hiding behind the apparent chaos of contemporary society. The cure is action and the creation of a new founding myth.

In this volume you will find different approaches to this cure in philosophical, political and transcendental declinations - not one denying the other, but intertwined in a solid, coherent whole.

This publication aims to make known outside Italy some of the most provocative and innovative minds that the non-conformist identitarian world has brought together over time, and this international edition has the ambition of bringing the ideas of the Italian vanguard back into the debate.

What is the Italian vanguard?

One of the authors of this volume says of certain "alternative" thinkers: « [...] they belong, both inwardly and in practice, to the monotheistic thought pattern, which makes them believe in the inevitability of the capitalist model»[1]. This statement is quite interesting if we look at the heated debate that has raged in the Italian identitarian world in recent years, when, after the global shock of the pandemic craze, anyone who said that a re-appropriation of technique was imperative was labelled "an-

---

[1]     F. Boco, *A Multidimensional View of Technique*, p. 94.

ti-traditional" or "a slave to the system". This happened for the very reason that Francesco Boco explained: many, too many, who thought they belonged to the world of identitarianism and non-conformism had already internalized the categories of thought of the opponent, creating dichotomies that were set in stone and could not be reconciled, and soon came to something that looked dangerously like neo-Luddism. Technology versus the ideal, ancient world; the purity of the Neolithic versus the horrors of the future; or, even more naively, the return to the opulent, carefree happiness of the 1980s. This shows, at the very least, a very poor ability to interpret history: and if you cannot interpret history, you cannot become history again.

The Italian vanguard presented in this volume boasts an impressive range of authors who, with their creative differences and similarities, fully embrace the European spirit: a spirit where opposites meet, where the vision of ancient fortresses overlaps with spaceships soaring into the interstellar void towards new worlds, where agriculture meets the most daring advances in bio-technology. A vision of power, myth and memory: a truly archeofuturistic tension that places our authors in a continuous line of thought that goes back to the daring exploits of Marinetti, Depero and the Italian futurists of the 1920s.

In this volume you will find deep reflections and powerful proposals on how to ride the tiger of history again, against those who envision its end:

Andrea Anselmo's profound excursus on the initiatory depth of Ernst Jünger's works and their connection with Guillaume Faye's magnum opus; Adriano Scianca's in-depth analysis of the concept of force and its philosophical and practical possibilities; Carlomanno Adinolfi on the need for a necessary reconciliation between what appears to be a dichotomy between barbarism and civilization; Guido Taietti on the war waged against heroism and the technological singularity happening today and how to make it ours; Francesco Boco on the deep meaning of interstellar exploration and the methodology to reclaim Technique as a purely Indo-European archetype.

These are oversimplified abstracts of the extensive material presented in this publication. We leave to the reader the adventure of diving in and making the best of all the powerful and eruptive material presented here, which we can further summarize as follows: We do not claim the past, but the meta-historical source of our identity. There is no static time where there is will to power, and past, present and future merge into a single sphere for those who dare to claim it.

Alberto Brandi

# Dynamis. A philosophy of force

*Adriano Scianca*

1. The history of European thought passes through some crucial historical turning points. One of these has to do with a word: *dynamis*. In the only passage of Plato known to us where there is a definition of the status of being, in the *Sophist*, the Greek philosopher hints at an ontology that he himself would later not delve into, preferring to carve out for himself, along with Aristotle, the role of the great normalizer of Greek thought. What, then, is being, *to on*? The Eleatic Stranger speaking in the Platonic dialogue states: *ouk allo ti plen dynamis*, nothing else than *dynamis*. Thus reads the whole passage: «I suggest that everything which possesses any power of any kind, either to produce a change in anything of any nature or to be affected even in the least degree by the slightest cause, though it be only on one occasion, has real existence For I set up as a definition which defines being, that is nothing else than power». To be is to produce or suffer an effect, to act or suffer. There is nothing else. What is real is a power that is exercised by producing effects. Indeed: what is real *is* these same effects. We are accustomed to thinking of force as an action of subject A on object B in order to

change its state of stillness or motion. This implies that first A and B exist and force would only occur later, if exerted at all. Instead, it is the force itself that defines A (as an acting entity) and B (as a suffering entity), who are merely the resultant of the forces that pass through them. And if the latter were not exerted, A and B simply would not exist. Ontology coincides with symptomatology. There is no upstream cause that might or might not discharge into a visible effect. As Nietzsche well explained.: «And just as common people separates lightning from its flash and takes the latter to be a *deed*, something performed by a subject, which is called lightning, popular morality separates strength from the manifestations of strength, as though there were an indifferent substratum behind the strong person which had the *freedom* to manifest strength or not. But there is no such substratum; there is no 'being' behind the deed, its effect and what becomes of it; 'the doer' is invented as an afterthought, - the doing is everything» (*On the Genealogy of Morality*, I, 13).

2. The translation of *dynamis* as "possibility," however, has steered Western thought toward a precise philosophical path. *Dynamis* understood in its original sense actually predates any division between power and act. It is an act/power that is not pre-oriented by some potentiality behind it that is, but may not be. Power is always at work: *en-ergheia*. Aristotle, on the other hand, thought of ontology according to the distinction between act and potency. Power in Aristotle is defined through its constitutive relation to non-power, the power-of-not. The proper consistency of power lies precisely in the fact that it can also fail to pass into the act, that it is power-of-not or even powerlessness (*adynamia*). At the heart of Western ontology is thus negation. Instead, we must rethink it as

pure affirmation, as a field of forces that cannot but exert themselves. *Physis* is composed of an infinite plurality of powers-acts that exert themselves, but these forces are precisely plural and in conflict with one another. They are so within us and outside us. When one force rules over another, the succumbing force aborts.What is possible is then the aborted forces themselves. Possibility is not an original given, but a derivative one. There is no power-of-not, there is the defeated power that cannot exert itself because it has been overwhelmed by another power. That is why the philosophy of forces is a thought of effectivity, not of possibility. The metaphysical mindset is desperately anchored in an idea of possibility as an exorcism of the real. It is convinced that multiple futures are enclosed in a "cabinet of possibilities" (Bergson) whose contents are known only to a select few. Similarly, compared to the past, metaphysics is obsessed with possibilities that have not become reality, because the real seems too arbitrary, too contingent, too random. That is why the metaphysician reads history as an archive of unrealized good intentions: real Christianity is not "real Christianity," the historical French revolution does not represent "the real ideals of revolution," realized communism does not reflect "real communism," the Italian resistance movement and '68 were "betrayed," and so on. Concrete history always disappoints metaphysical expectations; reality always has a somewhat fascist flavor. Precisely for this reason, metaphysics gives rise to an ethics of intentions: "Sure, communism caused millions of deaths, but its intentions were good". The philosophy of forces, on the other hand, is an ethics of effects: we are held accountable for the effects; there is no reality behind reality made up of pious hopes and good intentions, there is only the stark, icy face of reality.

3. If being is *dynamis*, reality is no longer made of substance, that is, of a fixed, solid element that remains identical to itself, but of force. This view coincides with the image of the world supported by the achievements of modern science, from electromagnetism to quantum physics, whereby there are no longer "things," but fields, relations, attractions, repulsions, co-implications. But it is the scientific-ontological view that the Dalmatian scholar Roger Boscovich had already realized in the 1700s (and which not coincidentally attracted Nietzsche's attention), according to which natural reality consisted of atoms understood as unextended points of force, and therefore devoid of any materiality, their essence exclusively determined by their dynamic relationship with other particles. For centuries it was believed that at the foundation of reality there were tiny bits of matter located at a single point in space and time. Today we know that, as we descend into the depths of the subatomic worlds, matter as we intuitively understand it ceases to exist, the boundaries and relationships between bodies take on a whole other dimension. At the bottom of reality, there is only force.

4. Force defines being; it constitutes its sole essence. In the Homeric texts it is said that Telemachus' *is* "listens to" and even "smiles at his father", that Hector's *menos* "falls swiftly toward the earth, into the dust," that Idomeneus' *sthenos* "turns to his attendant". These are all Greek terms for strength. The whole subject is here summarized and defined by force; force itself is the subject. Telemachus, Hector or Idomeneus are nothing but their force. Similarly, the limit of a thing is not the frame surrounding its figure, but the limit where the action stops. In his lectures on Spinoza, Gilles Deleuze gives the example of the forest. Gradually, the forest thins out and gives way to a clear-

ing. What is the boundary of the forest? Are there lines that mark its boundary? No, what defines the boundary is «the action of the forest, that is, the forest that had so much power of action reaches the limit of its power of action; it can no longer bite into the terrain, as it's thinning out. It's thinning out, and what reveals that this is not a contour is the fact that we cannot even specify the precise moment at which there is no more forest. Were you already inside the undergrowth? How did you pass from the forest into the undergrowth, and from the undergrowth into the thicket, all that? I mean, really, I don't need to force myself much to say: there was a tendency, and this time, the limit is not separable, a kind of tension towards the limit. This is a dynamic limit that is opposed to a contour-limit. The thing has no other limit than the limit of its power of action or of its action. The thing is thus power of action and not form. The forest is not defined by a form; it is defined by a power of action: power of action to create the trees all the way to the moment when it can no longer do so. Hence, the question that I have for the forest is not: what is your shape and what are your contours? The only question that I have for the forest is: what is your power of action? That is, how far will you go? » (*The Velocities of Thought*, Lecture 11).

5. The philosophy of forces also integrally rewrites the grammar of "spiritual" discourse, which is still almost always hinged on a naive and deceptive dualism: the "true world" and the "false world," "being" and "appearing," "Matrix" and "Zion," the world "at the bottom of the cave" and the world "in the sunlight," etc. Thus, there would be a dimension of objective and uncorrupted authenticity to which, after a suitable path, man could draw, leaving behind a world of illusory appearances.

But there is none of this: there is only the spiritual dimension that one has the strength to realize. Julius Evola understood this very well. The Italian thinker gives the example of two generic spiritual states, A, the condition of ordinary knowledge, and B, the state in which one accesses a different and deeper awareness of the world. Now, «suppose that state B is such that that a particular metaphysical reality already existed or was true in A, although the ego could not yet notice it. Will it be concluded from this that there was no real progress, no building up, but only a recognizing, a taking notion of what already was? Not at all: because this knowledge – that the object of *shruti* [divine revelation] already existed in A – belongs to state B, and yet it is something that would never have been realized if from A one had not gone all the way to B. [...] Can it then be said that B existed in the state of possibility or "in potency" in A? It cannot: since I can speak concretely of B as a possibility of A only if B has actually been realized». (*L'uomo come potenza*[1]). The multiple states of being are not a 10-story building which we simply have to climb, one that exists independently of us. Before we had access to a floor, it *did not exist*. It is the very power of man overcoming himself that defines the spiritual horizon of his domain. If the *Matrix* movie has thrilled us, it is not because it has shown us the "real world" in which a mixed-race humanity lives hidden underground like cockroaches, stirring up Old Testament symbolism, but because it has shown us the spark of an empowered existence here and now, in the only dimension that matters, the one where things really happen.6. In the philosophy of forces, the world is full, not empty. The interplay of forces leaves no empty space. This is also

---

1        (Translator's Note: *Man as Potency*. I have translated this excerpt as no published translation has been found).

true for man, who nevertheless is accustomed to thinking of himself in emptiness (indeed, as the very being suspended in emptiness and capable of looking into the face of emptiness) because of metaphysics. In the *Critique of Pure Reason*, Immanuel Kant posed his famous three fundamental questions, "What can I know?", "What must I do?", and "What can I hope for?" In a letter dated May 4, 1793, sent to Carl Friedrich Staudlin, he had added another one, which somewhat summarized the first three: "What is man?" And the reason for this convergence lies in the fact that all three questions presuppose a common character of the human being: that of non-immediacy, of division, of fracture, of estrangement. There is a distance between man and the world, an unbridgeable gulf, which is why he asks what he can know (immediate knowledge, that which comes from the senses, being fallacious by definition), what he should do (assuming that the actions to which he is led by inclinations are wrong), what he is allowed to hope for (since what gives value to life is supposed to be outside life, what justifies the world is supposed to be beyond the world). Instead, the philosophy of forces is a thought of immanence, immediacy, fullness. In fact, behind every "cultural" human practice lies the desire to regain that seemingly lost "naturalness". In art, in sport, in seduction, in dance, in ritual, in thought itself we see the attempt to bridge that hiatus between man and the world at work, to fit into a flow, to trigger an automatism in which everything comes of itself, without detachment, without effort, without reflection. When Eastern disciplines call for "emptiness" in the mind, the Westerner imagines some abysmal thought to be evoked. Actually that "emptiness" to be sought is a "fullness": it is about "emptying" the mind of everything that separates us from the thing, from the world. Armand Duplantis,

Olympic pole-vaulting champion, said in an interview, "When I jump it is as if my body takes over, a domination over the rest of myself. I don't have full perception, everything happens naturally like a flowing river." When we see Lionel Messi advancing with the ball at his feet, we do not perceive a soccer player-subject trying to control a ball-object which is ontologically different from him, we see the soccer player-ball node moving in unison, with immediacy, spontaneity. Everything happens in the flow.

7. All this also takes us past the great contemporary philosophical impasse between realism and constructivism, based on a distorted reading of the famous Nietzschean idea that "there are no facts, only interpretations". This phrase was mostly read as a denial of the "hard" character of certain aspects of the real, in favor of a general plasticity, a reduction of the factual to the linguistic. Which has exposed "postmodernists" to the obvious objection of "realists": why, in reading Nietzsche, can't you get through the walls? Why, in an Isis attack, do postmodernists die exactly like the others instead of "deconstructing" the linguistic game of the knife that is about to cut their throats? But interpretation, in Nietzsche, is not a linguistic, cultural practice; it is the natural movement of the will to power that characterizes all reality and outside of which nothing exists. It is the expansive action of the *natura naturans* that involves all being. It is free creation of forms and appropriation of other, already created forms, without ever being able to be traced back to a virgin original form, free from interpretation. In this sense, the fact that in empirical experience some interpretations "impose themselves" in a seemingly inescapable way does not testify at all to the existence of a supposed external world of objective facts, but only to a play of forces in

which the limitation of our force and the superior power of another force are revealed. Just to give an example, it can undoubtedly be dialectically effective to define sexual binarism as a non-deconstructible fact, according to a recurring conservative argument. Philosophically, however, what we must observe is that sexual binarism is a force that is imposed, that can be channeled (biological sexes are already always interpreted, never purely, a-culturally given) but around which a series of effects that are difficult to circumvent are knotted. Quite simply, the force of gender ideologies is not intense enough to override the force of sexual binarism, except in relative and marginal forms.

8. A political idea, an ideology, or a worldview imposes itself as strongly as the force that runs through it. The woke ideology imposes itself because it certainly shows force, even if it is largely illusory due to the elitist nature of its proposals and the support of many intellectual and media oligarchies. It can, however, be beaten only by a force of higher intensity. Conservatism, on the contrary, opposes woke ideology only by the force of inertia, the sheer permanence of an outdated status quo. By opposing progressive ideologies to a "normal" or "natural" world, conservatism postulates the existence of a taken-for-granted, a-historical, uninterpreted order removed from the domain of forces. But the force of inertia alone is not enough. On the contrary, it can even act as a regulating element for over-accelerated opposing forces: the conservative ends up being the one who makes the projects of the most unrestrained progressivism possible, imposing on them some "moderation" and in any case defending as "natural" the "subversions" of yesterday, which over time have become habits. Otherwise, con-

servatism is an exhausted philosophy through which no force passes. Opposing the new left requires more than nostalgia for the "good old days." It needs a more intense, more creative, more dynamic force. We will not be saved from the screaming activists with purple hair by model citizens with ties and white hair holding orations on "values." No revolution has ever been about values. Values are moral crystallizations suspended in mid-air, they have nothing of the instinctiveness of a real, carnal ethos, they are not children of the blood, the nerves, the heart. But neither do they have the imposing capacity of some "greater force." Values always recall a moment of weariness, a bloodless force. And, in fact, values are never enforced, they are always threatened. Before decaying, values do not exist. No society, in fact, is based on values but on a myth, a project, a necessity, even an interest, but never on values. Then when this driving force wanes, one fixes it in an immobile (and therefore fallacious) snapshot and invents that all this is a value. It is, in short, an ideological *a posteriori* construction, a moral arcadia built with hindsight. It is not with values that woke ideology will be defeated, but with the innocent force of a new myth and the fierce joy of the political soldiers who will be imbued with it.

9. Conservatism also errs when it wants to oppose progressive ideologies with "truth". The philosophy of forces does not demand to be recognized as "true," it does not claim that its arguments are "right," it does not intend to be "right." For it, there is no objective or universal criterion for establishing that one thesis is better than another, except precisely force. Not necessarily violent force, but also simply argumentative force, which, however, has nothing to do with asserting universal and rational valid-

ity. As Giuseppe Rensi writes: "Precisely because, from the rational point of view, contrasting theses of justice, opposing statements of law, have the equal suffrage of reason; precisely because therefore, all being truths, one cannot rationally establish which among them constitutes the truth; precisely therefore no rational solution is possible and the solution can only come from pure fact; from the extra-rational fact, from the fact of force, of *imperium*, of mere authority." (*La filosofia dell'autorità*[2]). In this sense, the philosophy of forces is nominalist, not essentialist. Categories are not "true" or "real" in themselves, but only insofar as they are traversed by a force. When Joseph De Maistre utters the manifesto phrase of nominalism, namely his famous maxim: «In my life I have seen Frenchmen, Italians, Russians, and so on. I even know, thanks to Montesquieu, that one can be Persian. But as for man, I declare I've never encountered him. », actually remains a middle way. Indeed, on closer inspection, the category of "French" is as much an abstraction as that of "man." What makes the one category "true" and the other "false" is the ability to pass through them a concrete force, giving real effects.

10. If there is no reason, if there is no universal point of view, how can we orient ourselves in the world? Nietzsche answers: through our taste. The German philosopher writes in *Thus Spoke Zarathustra*: «And ye tell me, friends, that there is to be no dispute about taste and tasting? But all life is a dispute about taste and tasting! Taste: that is weight at the same time, and scales and weigher; and alas for every living thing that would live without dispute about weight and scales and weigher!» ("The

---

2        (TN: *The Philosophy of Authority*. I have translated this excerpt as no published translation has been found).

Sublime Ones"). For Nietzsche, then, taste is at once weight (the object of evaluation), scale (the instrument of evaluation) and the one who weighs (the subject of evaluation). Indeed, the central role attributed to taste should not lead one to believe that it is the attribute of a tasting subject and that therefore everything is reduced, precisely, to a matter of subjective preferences. We are, in fact, as much the origin as the product of taste. We are already forever caught in a chain of taste that has no origin and no end, that runs through us, that defines us, and that we in turn relaunch and prolong. Moreover, this taste has nothing contemplative about it: it is an appropriation of being, a creative interpretation that conflicts with other interpretations - since there is nothing that has not been already interpreted, nothing virgin or neutral. It is well understood, then, as taste - interpretation - force. How is taste communicable, since it is not based on refutable rational arguments? Nietzsche again states: « How does the general taste alter? By the fact of individuals, the powerful and influential persons, expressing and tyrannically enforcing without any feeling of shame, their *hoc est ridiculum, hoc est absurdum*; the decisions, therefore, of their taste and their disrelish: —they thereby lay a constraint upon many people, out of which there gradually grows a habituation for still more, and finally a necessity for all. » (*The Joyful Science*).


11. If it is true that "man does not dispose of force. He is disposed of it" (Rocco Ronchi), then what about rationality, *ego cogito*, transparency to self, man's humanity? What about consciousness? Consciousness is an *organon*, that is, etymologically, a tool, a purely operational, functional device, slowly formed by evolution for eminently pragmatic purposes. And what is evolution if

not the resultant of the infinite forces that precede and pass through a body? Consciousness is an evolutionary weapon, which – moreover – is not an exclusive of man. And it is a weapon that is obscure, unclear and fleeting for man. There is nothing in consciousness that has to do with "truth" about oneself or the world. Nor anything to do with some universal, abstract, uniquely human rationality. Not surprisingly, the most recent studies tell us of an *embodied cognition*, which has always been inextricably linked to the body, to action, to movement, to doing. The eye does not see in the abstract, contemplating the world to acquire pure knowledge, but is always caught up in a vision-action dyad. Cognitive science tells us that vision and action are not two distinct faculties but two constituent parts of a single visuomotor world. As for consciousness as self-reflection, as man's questioning of man, it is nothing but a fold of that same instinctual, embodied, disseminated, active device we have been talking about so far. It is nothing ontologically different; it is just the same flow of force bending and reflecting itself. Once we understand this aspect of human consciousness, all the age-old moral questions about the possible consciousness of machines, which would be about to undermine an alleged moral primacy of homo sapiens, are dispelled. Consciousness is not an essence; it is something that functions in a certain way. And if therefore something functions exactly like a human consciousness, there is no reason to avoid considering it as a consciousness. Human primacy does not exist: there is a human perspective that meets, compares or clashes with animal, vegetable, mineral, alien, divine or digital perspectives.

12. The forces that pass through an organism are divided into active and reactive ones: the force that dominates,

determines the energy polarity of the organism. Active is that organism which acquires, dominates, grasps, conquers only to then give back, to make itself a "free creator of symbols," to build, to affirm itself. When this discharge mechanism works properly, when it is not blocked, there is positive polarity, there is affirmation, there is an active attitude. On the other hand, there is reaction when the mechanism is blocked and there is no possibility/willingness to release the excess energy in an ecstasy of overflowing joy. In this case there is re-sentment, which is the sentiment that stagnates, that rots, that causes infection. It is the echo of action that constantly comes back, it is resentment that, not finding an outlet, settles, ferments. Servile mentality dominates in an organism when reactive forces succeed in neutralizing active forces by making them in turn reactive. In a reactive organism, the reactive forces succeed in blocking the discharge mechanism and neutralizing the active forces. How? Through ideological, philosophical, linguistic, ethical and political moral-metaphysical paraphernalia. The bimillennial terrorist work devoted to devaluing existence, blaming man, and denigrating action aims at nothing but this. That between active spirit and reactive spirit is the real fundamental distinction between men, movements, civilizations, eras. By inhibiting the process of creation, reaction inevitably ends up dwelling on the already created, on the *done* rather than the *doing*. It is the abstract logos of which Giovanni Gentile spoke, the logos that focuses on what has already been thought rather than the thought in action. Here then is where the boulder of the past blocks the way to a full enjoyment of the present and any momentum towards the future. It is the cult of what-is-past denounced by Marinetti, the stale veneration of the greatness of the time that was that prevents the greatness of tomorrow's time. Being active also means knowing how to forget. The power of oblivion is underestimated.13. It is not man who makes strength, it is strength that makes man. But man can channel it through *askesis*. Which is not asceticism, in the sense of self-denial, saying no to life, but the exercise of force, the practice of force being self-disciplined and the selection of force itself. Man is a battlefield between opposing forces. When a force manages to win, to determine a hierarchy, then man is torn from the headless flow of forces and finds his ipseity. The "anthropological machine" (Agamben) at the bottom of this process of stripping away forces is training. Living is itself already training in an implicit way. But man has developed the ability to train himself explicitly and consciously, to construct himself in view of the goals he intends to achieve. Against Kant, it is a matter of making oneself a means and not an end, of bringing forth, as Simone Regazzoni puts it, "a radical form of affirmation of the singularity of the living body that is self-creating and more precisely hyper-creating (our improvement as continuous self-surpassing and vital enhancement is at stake) against all the forces of mediocrity that want to limit it, enslave it, homologate it, flatten it, decree what it can and cannot do, what it can and cannot be" *(Plato's Gymnasium*[3]). But, once he has learned to move himself, to domesticate himself, to train and nurture himself, man fatally ends up moving, taming, training, and nurturing others as well. As Foucault had realized, the government of self is always linked to the government of others. Training, understood in its ontological dimension related to the selection of forces, is not an innocent practice of self-improvement, but the antechamber of a radical an-

---

3        (TN: *Plato's Gymnasium*. I have translated this excerpt as no published translation has been found).

thropotechnics that contemporary humanism has tried, in vain, to remove.

# STAY SUPERHUMAN
## A short guide on how to find our roots in the will to power

*Carlomanno Adinolfi*

**Humans and Beasts.**

"Stay human." "We are all human beings." "Where has humanity gone?"

How many times have we heard this refrain, repeated in an outraged tone when specific news events have prompted the media and some political organizations to pass new laws in the name of, precisely, "humanity," as if just repeating it over and over again will bring the beasts, the ignorant, the populists towards gentler pursuits, that is, to think as they do. Yet the arrogance with which these people try to convert the masses to their word is only the tip of the iceberg, by far the least serious element of the issue. Instead, what should be alarming, what should put a clear dividing wall between these people and us, should be the very concept they try to preach. That is, that we should characterize ourselves not by our qualities, but solely as "human beings." For in the end, it is only in this way that we can truly be equal, stripping ourselves of all qualitative assertions and anything that they consider to be just a useless as well as harmful social construct, be it gender, ethnicity, roots, history, culture, artistic ability, and finally arrive at the most basic, raw and stripped-down nature: to simply be "human beings." This leveling that wants to reduce Man solely to a biological specimen of his species can also be seen in many social memes, which even in their basic elementary nature only highlight this drift. It is full of rather idiotic pictures (*the left can't meme...*) with identical skulls or skeletons placed in a row and under each of them the ethnic specification. The meaning is clear: racial, ethnic, gender diversity is just an illusion because at the end of the day, but only at the end of the day, when you reduce man to the bone, to his mere elementary mechanical structure, we are all the same. Some time ago another meme was going around with two people kissing visualized in x-rays and of whom, therefore, only the skeleton is visible. A beautiful image, according to the "humanitarians," because it is not clear from it whether they are a man and a woman or two people of the same sex, and even better, it is not clear what race/ethnicity they are, because after all, they are just "human beings who love each other."

Beyond the typical ignorance of the arrogant, allegedly cultured and self-declared educated midwits who usually characterize this category of people – because any scholar in the field could tell the sex, ethnicity and age of the find just from a skeleton or from a skull (thus screwing up even this last vague wish for equality) – here again what is alarming is the reduction of Man to a mere mechanical specimen of a species. At this point, when one is reduced not even to the simple biological level – never mind the obvious biological differences! – but even to the mechanical level, one does not even understand why one should boast about being differentiated from beasts. And here then comes the moral issue: to "be human" one must have "human feelings." And thus, we enter the worst and most cloying vortex of goodness, moralism and pietism typical of a certain trinitarian and fanatical progressivism. In essence, anyone who is not "good" like the Democrats is an animal. And as such must be re-educated, or confined if not physically put down if the re-education practice fails.

A sentiment typical of a certain left whose genesis is found in postwar anti-fascism and which over the years has matured, or perhaps rotted, into woke ideology. In Italy we have Elio Vittorini[1]'s infamous novel *Uomini e no*[2] written in 1945 at the end of World War II. The title refers precisely to a distinction between those who can be considered men (obviously the partisans) and those who do not even have the right to be considered as such (the fascists). This moral division would not only remain entrenched in the left for a long time, but would even become its very ideological core. In the 70s, when in Italy we had the so-called Years of Lead[3], a major leftist motto was 'Killing a fascist is not a crime', precisely because fascists, or rather anyone who could be accused of being a fascist, was not worthy of even the most basic civil rights. A motto that was not just empty words but had concrete effects when anti-fascists took to killing even young MSI[4] militants or

---

1	Elio Vittorini, 1908-1966, Italian writer who switched from fascism to communism in 1942 and then to the Italian Resistance in 1943, adhering to the intransigent anti-fascist line. He was one of the leading Italian intellectuals after World War II.

2	English edition: *Men and not Men*, Marlboro Press 1985.

3	The years between the end of the 1960s and the beginning of the 1980s in Italy, characterized by an extremization of the political dialectic that produced street clashes, armed struggle and terrorism

4	Movimento Sociale Italiano (*Italian Social Movement*), Italian party founded in 1947 by veterans of the Italian Social Republic.

their families[5] in cold blood. Yet this motto echoes still today: let us just think how journalists have defended the activist Ilaria Salis[6], who cannot be considered guilty as she would have targeted "just neo-nazis" who, therefore, can just be killed on the streets with no regrets whatsoever. But let us now gloss over this fact, as well as over the fact that the "humanitarian goodness" of these people actually hides an ancestral hatred that almost always results in dreaming of an Orwellian world of thought control, house-to-house preventive arrests and Siberian mass re-educations. Let us also admit that these people really are good, that they are driven by real feelings of universal piety that urge the good of humanity understood as above. But even in this case, perhaps especially in this case, one must emphatically reject the need to "be human." If the ultimate goal is to be some kind of parody of a medieval Morality Play with a skull reminding us that in the face of death we are all equal and the only thing that matters is "being good" because everything else, such as courage, strength, wisdom, will to power and affirmation is just vanity, then perhaps it is better to be something else and be considered beasts.

---

5       Infamous is the fire of Primavalle, a working-class neighborhood in Rome where, on 16 April 1973, an arson attack by militants of the extremist Potere Operaio formation led to the death of a 22-year-old young man and a 10-year-old boy, sons of the secretary of the local MSI section. The killers were aided and abetted in their escape by well-known Italian intellectuals and journalists.

6       Ilaria Salis, a member of the German anti-fascist terrorist organization Hammerbande, arrested on February 11, 2024 for armed assaults on Hungarian citizens believed to be far-right militants or sympathizers. Hammerbande's assaults in those days included ordinary bystanders mistaken for "fascists." She was elected MEP in the ranks of the left-wing Italian party AVS, obtaining parliamentary immunity thanks to which she was released from prison

## Superhumanism vs Egalitarianism

In 1982 Giorgio Locchi[7] published the book *Nietz-sche, Wagner e il mito sovrumanista*[8]. In it Locchi affirmed the so-called open theory of history, according to which becoming is always characterized by a conflict between worldviews or "tendencies." What is unfolding before our eyes is the conflict between egalitarianism and superhumanism. Needless to say, the moralistic tendency that puts the "humanitarian" sentiment above all else in order to affirm an equality that succeeds where even biology cannot reach is the prerogative of the former. Which of course rejects any kind of "fierce" tendency that can lead to the affirmation of differentiating qualities. Better to live a hundred years as a sheep than one day as a lion [9], the lion itself must instead be exterminated for the sake of the species. If we look closely, we are witnessing a great attempt to repress all the "fierce" qualities of the human being. A man who is too masculine is undoubtedly a "toxic male chauvinist"; a womanizer who behaves like Sean Connery's James Bond or Alain Delon is a sexual predator and perhaps a potential rapist[10]; a child who stands up to the bully by beating him up instead of reporting him

---

7      Giorgio Locchi, 1923-1992. Italian journalist who during his work as a correspondent in Paris met Alain de Benoist, with whom he was among the founders of GRECE and Nouvelle Droite, still recognized as among the leading think tanks of the European radical and revolutionary right.

8      *Wagner, Nietzsche and the Superhumanist Myth*, still untranslated in English (TN).

9      "It is better to live one day as a lion than a hundred years as a sheep", motto of Italian soldiers on the frontline during World War I and later often quoted by Benito Mussolini.

10      In 2021 Carey Fukunaga, director of "007 No Time to Die", called Sean Connery's 007 a rapist. After Alain Delon's death, feminist journalist Nicoletta Verna called his beauty "unbearable" and bearer of a "questionable model of masculinity".

to the teacher is punished more severely than the bully himself; a street fight, especially if it happens for political reasons and one dares to have "certain ideas," is likely to be punished with a disproportionate number of years in prison. And, who knows, this is the path followed, if only unconsciously, by all the latest crazy vegans and environmentalists  that blame hunting, horse racing, bullfighting and even eating meat and any animal product. Then again, what is the point of rehabilitating or even proudly reaffirming the "ferocity" typical of predatory beasts? To do so now in this age has the flavor of insanity, of dangerous psychopathy even. But it is only so because we are indoctrinated from childhood in egalitarian morality. They will have you believe that reaffirming the ferocity of the predator has only to do with a sadistic taste for blood, with senseless violence as an end in itself, with "supremacist" instincts of abuse, with a bestial tendency that the evolution of mankind should have overcome and erased. But this is not the case.

The reality is that the standard bearers of "do-gooder" egalitarianism fear and viscerally hate those ancestral instincts that since the dawn of Man have always characterized the warrior drive towards struggle and victory, instincts that has always been the defining factor of nobility and thus has always elevated the *aristoi*[11] above the masses. In them we have the echo of Nietzche's words, in whom, along with Wagner, Locchi identified the genesis of the superhumanist trend of the last two centuries: "At the centre of all these noble races we cannot fail to see the beast of prey, the magnificent blond beast avidly prowling round for spoil and victory; this hidden centre needs release from time to time, the beast must out

---

11      ἄριστοι, a Greek term literally meaning "the best", hence the term *aristocracy*.

again, must return to the wild: – Roman, Arabian, Germanic, Japanese nobility, Homeric heroes, Scandinavian Vikings – in this requirement they are all alike "[12].

## Only the predator can carry the Fire

However, bringing back the wild instinct of the beast of prey does not possess a uniquely aristocratic significance. Think of all the great civilizations: the Germanic one arose from Norse raiders, pirates and predators; the Greek one was born from the great Achaean and Mycenaean invaders; Rome was born thanks to a band of raiders; the Empire of Japan was born from the clash of clans led by raiding warriors; Vedic India and Persia were born thanks to the Aryan invaders. Civilization arises only from predators. And this certainly does not only apply to the ancient world. The last great European nations were born thanks to the *Sturm und Drang* and the Romantic spirit that reaffirmed, again, the heroic impulse. United Italy came into being thanks to the *Risorgimento*, which was led by Garibaldi, called a pirate and a raider by his detractors who evidently do not realize that they were honoring him with these terms, and it was thanks to a pirate expedition that he successfully overcame bureaucratic and diplomatic agreements[13].

The German nation was born thanks to the Prussian war machine. And the whole Romantic spirit was born thanks to Napoleon, who was primarily a conqueror. If we also think of the epic of the United States, it was born

---

12      F. Nietzche, *On the Genealogy of Morality*, Cambridge 2006, p. 23.

13      The Expedition of the Thousand through which, in 1861, Garibaldi succeeded in achieving the unification of Italy, effectively blew up the negotiating table by which the then Piedmontese prime minister, Cavour, was seeking a federation of Italian states under French and Austrian sponsorship. Instead, Garibaldi's action led to full independence and autonomy, taking all other actors by surprise.

out of the myth of the frontier where the protagonists were in fact raiding adventurers in search of new lands. The egalitarian myths themselves, from the French Revolution to the Russian Revolution, were born in terror, savagery and bloodshed. And the current democratic set-up cannot live without constant conflict and raids on those with resources or those at important strategic junctions. Egalitarianism *per se*, the "bleeding heart", "humanity" have never created anything. Creation, genesis, presupposes an affirmation, be it of a principle, a people, a caste or a clan. A founding myth is always needed. And myth is *epos* and there is no *epos* without a struggle.

The ability of predators to beget and give life is something that has also been found in nature. It has been noted how the 1995 reintroduction of wolves, which had been missing in the area since the 1920s, revitalized Yellowstone Park by profoundly changing its entire ecosystem: by hunting deer and other herbivores, wolves caused their decline, which led to the growth of plants and trees, such as aspens and willows, previously endangered by too many herbivores. The growth of plants led to the flowering of fruits that attracted insects and birds but also otters, beavers and other rodents. The decrease in coyotes due to the arrival of wolves brought back rabbits and mice and with them their natural predators, such as foxes and eagles. In this new balance new species of animals and plants have thrived, and the increase in vegetation has decreased soil erosion, riverbanks have strengthened and their courses have stabilized. There is no life except in struggle. As the Greek philosopher Heraclitus said, "Polemos pater panton," conflict is the father of all things. A herd can never create anything; it is only the pack that can give birth to something. And no pack of wolves can ever be as destructive as a herd of "good" herbivores. That is why, when we find ourselves in a tired, decadent, mortiferous age that seems to be unable to generate anything anymore, just as the present age is, it is necessary to rediscover the spirit of ferocity, to rediscover the momentum of barbarism, to renew the vitality of the first fire bearers who ignited civilizations.

## The balance between Barbarism and Civilization

When the barbaric and ferocious instinct of the predator fails, when it subsides due to "too much civilization", death comes. Man debases himself and loses manhood, the wolf disappears and the reign of coyotes, jackals and the life-devouring herd returns. Konrad Lorenz[14], considered the father of ethology before political correctness made him a victim of cancel culture, claimed that the greatest risk to humanity were not wars, diseases or famine as much as the decline and loss of more specifically human qualities. And by human qualities he certainly did not mean those of the "humanitarians" standard bearers of egalitarianism but just the opposite. "The human spirit then rendered natural selection inoperative, because it succeeded in virtually completely eliminating all hostile influences from the outside world[15]".

When, in short, man no longer has to hunt, when he no longer has to deal with risk, when from a wolf he turns into a house dog, he is destined to decline. Along the same lines, though starting from totally different analyses, comes American writer Jack Donovan. He

14      Konrad Lorenz, 1903-1989, Austrian ethologist founder of Austrian ethology. He was an inconvenient figure for having joined the German National Socialist Party in 1940 and for his active presence on the Eastern Front, where he was taken prisoner by the Soviets.

15      K. Lorenz, *The Waning of Humaneness*, Little Brown 1987. I have translated this excerpt myself as I was not able to refer to the English edition of the book (TN).

states: "Human masculinity is the evolutionary product of gang selection — of bands of men who hunted and fought their way through far more perilous and demanding ages. Human masculinity — the testing and proving of strength, courage, mastery and the desire to earn the respect of a given group of men — requires conflict to thrive, but also to survive. Eternal peace is the death of manliness. The peace sign is a death rune"[16]. And: "Human masculinity is a hypertrophic development of the body and psyche in response to external pressure—to the looming threats of predation, intergroup conflict, environmental stress, and resource scarcity. In the absence of external pressure, masculinity either fails to develop in the first place, or slowly atrophies. When people wonder if the men of their age are less manly — farther from the "most-masculine" — than the men who preceded them, this absence of development is generally explained by a corresponding absence of pressure[17]".

Donovan calls this particular era, dominated by feminism and male devirilization values, the Empire of Nothing. The only way not to become extinct is to rediscover the Way of Men by returning to a concept of absolute masculinity: "Manly virtues should be virtues directly related to manhood. The virtues that men all over the world recognize as manly virtues are the fighting virtues. Epics and action movies translate well because they appeal to something basic to the male condition — a desire to struggle and win, to fight for something, to fight for survival, to demonstrate your worthiness to other men. The virtues associated specifically with being a man outline a rugged philosophy of living — a way to be that is also a strategy for prevailing in dire and dangerous times. The

16        J. Donovan, *Becoming a Barbarian*, Dissonant Hum 2016.

17        J. Donovan, *A More Complete Beast*, Dissonant Hum 2018.

Way of Men is a tactical ethos. If you are fighting to stay alive and you are surrounded by potential threats, what do you need from the men fighting with you? What do you need from us to fend off them? If eating means facing danger together, who do you want to take with you? What virtues do you need to cultivate in yourself and the men around you to be successful at the job of hunting and fighting??"[18].

For Donovan, the Way of Man leads to gathering in gangs, in bands, in communities of brothers who, compared to the Empire of Nothing, must be considered barbarians, outcasts, bearers of values adverse to the present civilization. The importance of barbarism as the "cradle" of man's vital and creative qualities is also found in R.E. Howard, the man who invented the world's most famous literary barbarian. The whole saga of Conan the Cimmerian is centered on the anthropological diversity between the "foreign" barbarian who meets hypercivilized kingdoms and the aristocrats, intellectual priests, and bureaucratic officials who carry on so-called civilization. The "bestiality" of Conan, deemed a ferocious animal by civilians, will turn out to be far more humane than the qualities displayed by the reigning bureaucrats. Famous is Conan's statement in one of the stories in the saga: "«Barbarism is the natural state of mankind», the borderer said, still staring somberly at the Cimmerian. «Civilization is unnatural. It is a whim of circumstance. And barbarism must always ultimately triumph»"[19]. Yet if civilization must not to kill barbarism, barbarism cannot remain an end in itself. Its strength lies precisely in being able to carry the flame of Fire that creates a clan

---

18    J. Donovan, *The Way of Men*, Dissonant Hum 2012.

19    R.E. Howard, *Beyond the Black River*, Weird Tales (May-June)1935.

around it and that is the seed of civilization. If barbarism does not create civilization, it is nothing but a sterile animal herd. Man remains an incomplete beast. How to harmonize these two tendencies without one bringing death to the other?

Adriano Scianca[20] has excellently faced the problem in his *Contro l'eroticamente corretto* [21]. He states: "Man, for his part, loves more to found civilizations than to abide by their laws. His element is that moment halfway between chaos and order that lies at the origin of society, the moment which Pascal and Montaigne called mystical, in which law is founded from nothing. The male finds himself in those historical passages that he eternally renews with wars and revolutions. If subjected too long to a given order, he withers, experiences the Freudian discomfort of civilization. This is why the tendency to gather in a Männerbund, a manly community: gangs, gangs, militias, fraternities, squads manifests itself so often in history [...] Of course, the gang clashes with another symbolic form of man's power: fatherhood. That is, the Law, the rules of the city. The band of brothers thrives where the father is missing, no longer there or not there yet, thus at the beginning or the end of civilization. When the father is there and performs his function, the brothers feel like sons first and foremost, the bond with the father prevails over that with each other. In order not to wither, civilization must hold the two dimensions together. If the gang prevails, it is anarchy; if the father dominates, it is an oppressive power that stifles individuality.

---

20      Adriano Scianca, Italian writer and journalist, one of the main cultural promoters of the CasaPound Italia movement and one of the founders of Prometheica, a magazine that promotes a proactive and heroic vision in its approach to the future and technology.

21      *Against the Erotically Correct*, still untranslated in English (TN).

The gang must be organically integrated into the Law[22]". This is something we find in all the great mythologies of our tradition. The clash between the Asi, the celestial gods of the nomadic warrior-hunter tribes, and the Vani, the chthonic fertility gods of the peaceful settled farmers, must be resolved in a covenant of coexistence and harmony in order to establish Norse civilization. In Rome, the same clash is found in the war between the founding core of Latin breeders and hunters, originally raiders and warriors led by Romulus, and the land- and agriculture-bound Sabines. The Rape of the Sabine women perpetrated by the early Romans should lead to a pact of harmony between the two components that would result in the Sabine king Titus Tatius reigning jointly with Romulus. Also in Rome there was a kind of ambivalence of the god Mars, the Mars Pater considered to be the father of Romulus' lineage: Mars in his full manifestation was the god of war, the one who had led the hunter raiders to found the new civilization and who accompanied them on raids outside the *pomerium*, the sacred boundary. But inside reigned Quirinus, for many a deified Romulus who represented the peaceful and "civilized" aspect of Mars himself.

The Roman archetype, in short, had to find the balance between the two drives. This is an aspect also present in more modern "foundations." If America was born in the myth of the frontier and the spirit of adventure yearning to push further and further west to face and conquer the unknown, so goes the myth of the ranch, of transforming the wild chaos of the new lands into an orderly space where a family can be built. But just as the ranch myth is needed not to turn the cowboy into an outlaw wanderer, the cowboy must keep being one on the ranch as well.

22    Adriano Scianca, *Contro l'Eroticamente Corretto*, Altaforte 2017.

Similarly, the two great revolutions of the 20th century, the fascist and communist revolutions, gave rise to the two myths of the Continuous Revolution and the Permanent Revolution, respectively. However, if the latter, theorized by Lev Trotsky, has more of an aspect of terrorist subversion to keep the preconditions to keep the revolutionary fires ablaze, the former, theorized by Mussolini, aims instead at keeping active that spirit defined as "mystical" by Montaigne and Pascal in the context of building a civilization and a New Man, endeavor that could never be considered accomplished. "Every revolution has three stages: it begins with the mystical, it continues with the policy, you end up with the administration. When a revolution becomes an administration, one can say it's over, liquidated[23]".

The two tendencies must therefore coexist, pushing and pulling each other. At one time this was accomplished by having the warrior aristocracy hold the positions of power and government. Only those who had the nature of the predatory wolf in them and knew the ferocity of battle and the will to fight, win and conquer and then experienced "the homecoming" without losing the vitalist momentum of the battlefield could lead other men. Quoting again Mussolini, "One can go from the tent to the palace provided one is prepared to go from the palace to the tent". If you leave leadership to the bureaucrats, that is the end. In the 4th century, Emperor Constantine canceled military service from the political *cursus honorum*. To become a magistrate, governor, senator, one no longer had to go serve in the legions. As a result, a resident army of barbarians was formed, which was no longer bound to the fortunes of Rome, and the

---

23      Sentence uttered by Mussolini on October 18, 1939 to the leadership of the School of Fascist Mysticism.

formation of a class of soft and fearful bureaucrats. In fifty years, the invincible machine of Rome would turn into a sieve and the first barbarians would sack the *Urbe*. A century later the entire empire would collapse and end.

## Death to conservatism

The necessary co-existence of these two tendencies, these two "ancestral drives" that must balance and maintain civilization, must not, however, lead to the misunderstanding of suggesting the democratic practice of alternating between conservatives and progressives. As for the progressivism typical of the "democratic" left, it is rather easy to note the total absence of that typical feral drive of the wolf archetype, necessary precisely for the gangs and bands that carry the creative fire with them. The "humanist" and humanitarian rhetoric that seeks to suppress if not eradicate the barbaric nature of man is in fact, as we have previously said, a founding core of the left that calls itself more progressive. So-called progressivism then has nothing of the adventurous spirit as much as it is a continuous subversive attempt to erode every achievement, in the pure Trotskyist spirit of permanent revolution.

Behind buzzwords such as progress, moving forward, winning new freedoms and rights, in fact, is now not even too covertly hidden the continuous attempt to disintegrate every bond necessary for the "way of men": family, clan, people, borders, identity. For this reason, especially in recent years, many militants, intellectuals or even simply part of the side that, depending on the years and latitudes, takes on the most diverse names - nationalists, identitarians, sovereignists, national-revolutionaries, non-conformists, alt-right and so on - have believed well to fight progressivism by fully embracing the ideas of conservatism. Although it is often - but not always - understandable to prefer a more conservative party, candidate, or president over those of the democratic, socialist, social democratic left, etc., to end up openly taking sides and fully espousing their ideology represents a mistake that is at once tactical, strategic, and above all ideal that can only lead to death. During a discussion involving Prometheica [24] I used the sarcastic phrase - but I am pretty sure I in turn heard it from someone else to whom I cede the copyright -"Conservatives are nothing more than the progressives of 20 years ago."

Think about it: those who want to "preserve the values" of today are merely defending values that were won, affirmed or imposed by progressives a few decades earlier and which conservatives of that time abhorred as degeneracy. The conservative is none other than the one who exclaims, "My lady, what a time! And to think that in my day..." without remembering that "in his day" there was an old conservative asshole who stated exactly the same thing. And so on backwards. And so, the conservative ends up idealizing a recent past, almost always coincidentally coinciding with the happy years of his childhood or adolescence, as a kind of golden age destroyed by the perfidious progressives. It's a bit like the parody of the Amish prayer in the Family Guy show, in which the old community leader says: "Although humans have been around for a million years, you feel strongly that they had just the right amount of technology between 1835 and 1850." Very often we hear a conservative dialectical fraud, that stated that they do not want to idealize the past or turn back the hands of time at all but that they want to "defend and thus preserve eternal values." But what, then, are these "eternal values" in the end? Even the left, when

---

24      See footnote 20.

it invents a new right to defend in order to destroy our identity, uses the same terms, saying it wants to assert "inalienable rights" that it has overnight baptized as such. In an article from December, Adriano Scianca stated:

"An angry and impoverished population, increasingly polarized and frustrated, is thus being asked to line up behind the "mobilizing" banners of conservation. Conservation of what? Of the very structures and institutions that have exploited and impoverished it? I know the refrain: the true conservative does not stand in defense of yesterday's world, but of eternal values. Even putting aside any philosophical misgivings about such a concept, my impression is that in any case these "eternal values" have a certain tendency to be embodied in clearly identifiable structures in the here and now and that therefore we then end up squaring off around the Church, the carabinieri, actionist patriotism[25], to the middle-class family, to the free market. Moreover, the belated discovery of conservatism entails the renunciation of any original declination of modernization. Not that conservatives necessarily have to live in caves. But by that name they are necessarily destined to live and embody the modernization of others, modernity declined according to progressive narratives and ideologies. And in fact, the right has almost everywhere been a vector of bad modernization and uprooting development (so much for "eternal values")"[26].

Maybe someone will tell you about the values of the ancestors, the need to have to "live like our grandpar-

---

25    The reference here is to the Action Party, which was founded in 1942 and brought together several non-Communist and non-Catholic anti-fascist formations

26    Social network post then published on the website of the Primato Nazionale magazine on December 7, 2021.

ents," someone else will talk about the Roman concept of *mos maiorum*, that is, the customs of the ancestors. Too bad this term indicates anything but what these conservatives claim.

Living like our ancestors does not mean dressing in bowler hats, monocle and a cane instead of ripped jeans, nor it does mean letting one's children play with educational wooden toys instead of video games, nor to reject technological and cultural innovations because they are considered dangerous to a "way of life that we must defend" (any reference to the Dodo in the animation film Ice Age is purely coincidental...). When Shinzo Abe was criticized for going, as prime minister, to the infamous Yasakuni Temple, known because it houses the ashes of all Japanese combatants who fell between the Meiji Renewal and 1945 and, therefore, also those of many convicted war criminals and for this haunt of Japanese nationalists and right-wing extremists, he firmly replied: "I went in order to have my ancestors judge my work". This is the meaning of *mos maiorum*, which is to live in such a way that the heroes of the past can consider us worthy of them.

At the entrance to the Redipuglia War Memorial, where Italian soldiers of the Great War are buried, a marble stele bears the inscription, "Not curiosity to see, but may the drive to be inspired lead you." Those who want to honor their ancestors must be inspired by their heroic deeds. It is also the meaning of the poet Simonides' epitaph carved at Thermopylae: "Go and report to the Spartans, wayfarer, that obedient to their Law we here lie."". Obeying the Law means acting heroically, inspired by the heroes of the past, so that we can in turn inspire our children and descendants. In fact, "living as our ancestors lived" is something absolutely antithetical to remaining static, moderate and reluctant to change. Instead, it implies always keeping alive that warrior, aristocratic, predatory component of Nietzsche's triumphant blond beast, of Howard's barbarian, of Donovan's more complete beast.

That component that led the original gang to build our benchmark civilization and that must not be dormant or put to sleep by "too much civilization." It is to live remembering that "You can go from the tent to the palace as long as you are ready to go from the palace to the tent." It is the meaning of the archaic Roman huts preserved for centuries on the Palatine Hill that reminded Roman magistrates and leaders that Rome was founded by a band of hunter herders and raiders ready to dismantle and rebuild with logs their dwellings to assault new lands and settle there. If we want to return to the concept of balance between the two forces, the dynamic one of the wolf, the gang and the conquest, and the static one of civilization that has to rein in the barbaric impetuosity so that it does not overreach and degenerate civilization into anarchy, honoring the spirit of the ancestors is more about the first component. It is something that reminds us, in the midst of civilization, that we must not lose our nature. It is something that drives us to new conquests, new challenges and, if that is not possible, to create new civilizations by always carrying with us the example of our Ancestors, as in the myth of Aeneas or the rite of *ver sacrum*[27].

The memory of ancestors makes sense only if it is projected into the future. If it stays anchored in the cult of the past, it would be merely a funeral commemoration. Now let us stop for a moment and consider explaining these

---

27      The Sacred Spring (*Ver Sacrum* in Latin) was a ritual commonly practiced by several Italic peoples that involved the migration of part of a community in order to establish new colonies.

things to an ordinary conservative of today: it is obvious that his reaction would be to see them all as dangerous, as degeneration, as anarchy, as a danger to the institutions he defends. And that is the great deception.

The conservative in the end is nothing but the weak face of the defense of the egalitarian status quo, of that Empire of Nothing that wants to kill man and his will to power, to heights, to conquest. If the progressive wants to do so because he sees in the "blond beast" the arch-enemy of the world he has built, the conservative does so because he is a fearful moderate who prefers the values imposed by the progressive but in a sugar-coated, mitigated way. And at the end of the day, should it come to a real clash between a worldview as dangerous as the superhumanist, barbaric and heroic one and the egalitarian one, rest assured that the conservative will have no doubts and will side with the latter along with the progressive, perhaps in the name of the common values of democracy or anti-fascism. Then there will be those who will tell you that we are now at the limit, that progressivism has gone too far, that we are at a moment of rupture where we have to take sides and defend whatever good still exists. But this is also a form of control. If we really were at such a point in history, close to an epochal zero, why would we limit ourselves to defending what was good in the old world instead of building a new one? As Donovan writes, "The collapse may be imminent and its doomsayers may be vindicated, but waiting for the world to start is not the same as starting it" [28]. Again, the conservative acts only as feedback in a system that seeks to regulate itself. Complex dynamic systems, whether biological or mechanical, in attempting to regulate themselves "dampen" certain behaviors so that their

______________

28      J. Donovan, *Becoming a Barbarian* op. cit.

output does not become unstable, so that the system always remains controlled. The conservative, if progressivism goes too far, merely stands in defense of a more dated, more moderate, less problematic progressivism in an attempt to defend that same mechanism that keeps both alive. While the progressive is the sworn enemy who wants to kill the noble predator, the conservative is the control valve that seeks to tame and depower it.

**Let us build a new myth for a new world**

Okay but then what to do? Would it not be better to try and put a stop to degeneration than to let everything go downhill? In fact, progressives themselves, left to act freely, deflagrate their contradictions and their inability to create anything much more than when they are restrained. Indeed, if restrained they push even harder on their battles. This, if nothing else, have been the teachings of the woke trend that exploded in reaction to Trump's election and that suddenly seems to be in reflux after four years of loose reins in which the woke-ists have generated only revulsion from almost the entire Western population as well as economic disasters for those who financed their projects. But I do not want to dwell on "accelerationist" theses that are not for everyone and that perhaps I do not espouse completely either. Let us assume that the moment asks for a tactical advantage in siding with the conservative parties. We must not forget what is being done: a tactical choice, precisely. Not an ideological one. The worst thing one could do would be just to give in ideologically, perhaps to seem more presentable, perhaps because the balance of power may discourage people and one sees more immediate or within reach results by giving in one's principles. Those who do so bring defeat within; those who do so are giving up on building a new world and have given in and now defend the world they wanted to fight, accepting its seemingly less grim aspects. Those who do so carry the desert within themselves. One must never, however, abandon the spirit of conquest.

Entering into dialectics with conservatives only makes sense if you have advantages, and that only happens if you can impose your keywords. If we want to assert the wholesome ferocity of the blond beast, we must be the noble conquerors, the elite who look down with aristocratic contempt on the self-righteous moderates and push them to be better by leading by example. Using the concept of the Overton Window so dear to many, we must make sure that the people with whom we are conversing are not, as always, the force that restrains the radical or unthinkable concepts of progressives to make them acceptable, but rather the ones who make acceptable and then popular our buzzwords that were unthinkable to all until yesterday, but which in fact hide a heroic and "incorrect" drive that many would like to find again. To mobilize in a sterile and immovable force, to sow in order to realize that "transvaluation of values" of which Nietzsche spoke.

Donovan's words are relevant: "It will be tempting to say that everything is wrong, that the world is evil, that there are fiendish degenerates ruining everything, stopping you from doing what you want to do — what you believe you should rightfully do. As you writhe and struggle on your knees, gnashing your teeth, your face red with indignation, it will be tempting to say that YOU are the victim — that YOU are the one being oppressed. Here lies The Trap. [...] The whole world, in fact, seems to be upside-down, crazy and ruled by the wicked. And it may seem that nothing good can be achieved until somehow, someday, the world is turned right-side-up again. [...] a more Noble approach to a desire for change is to take on the mindset of the conqueror. The conqueror creates change according to his liking, and it is good and right because he likes it — because he willed it — not because of any theoretically objective sense that it is morally good or evil. The revolutionary wants to "fix" the world by turning the moral wheel one way or the other, while the conqueror creates the world he wants"[29]. How to do it? How to mobilize an environment that seems by its very nature stuck in reaction? Only Polemos is *pater panton*: new challenges must be issued, for only the willingness to embrace challenges and overcome them can lead man to regain his nobility. And how to do this now, when there are no longer great spaces to conquer, that there is no frontier beyond which to venture, that there are no great Indo-European migrations through which to impose oneself? Let us recall the words of Fight Club: "We're the middle children of history, man. No purpose or place. We have no Great War. No Great Depression. Our Great War's a spiritual war... our Great Depression is our lives."

A titanic challenge, taking up the challenge where there seems to be only nothingness. But paradoxically a nothingness that, precisely as such, offers enormous potential. "The Empire of Nothing has created an emptiness where anything can happen, where magic and creation can happen — a new Ginnungagap[30]. If you found yourself in the void with your brothers before the monstrous body of a dead god, what kind of world would you build from his corpse?[31]". Here is our task, to imagine the world

---

29      J. Donovan, *A More Complete Beast*, Dissonant Hum 2016.

30      In Norse cosmogony, Ginnungagap is the primordial void from which the two poles that will give birth to the cosmos emerge.

31      J. Donovan, *Becoming a Barbarian*, op. cit.

we want and make it the new mobilizing myth. Our challenge must be to create epic and heroic narratives that awaken man's natural urge to be himself and counter the utilitarian and moralistic narratives of conservatives or the dystopian and fanatical narratives of progressive egalitarians. How? Examples are endless. AI is a trendy topic today. Progressives want to use it to mechanize and dehumanize humans hoping for the utopia in which machines will rid us of racism and intolerance – which means: making sure that anyone who does not follow the algorithm is eliminated?

Fuck then those who say that AIs are dangerous, the devil's weapon, Skynet and bullshit, let us imagine what differentiated men with great abilities like a Caesar or Alexander the Great could do if they had a very powerful AI at their disposal. "Interstellar travel and space missions are just a waste of resources that could be devoted to something else, what good are they?" We care nothing about what is useful; space is our new frontier, the place of our next *ver sacrum*. Could it be that the civilizations and discoveries made by the greats of the past were made only after adventurers, conquerors and pioneers wondered what their adventure was for, or did they set out for the sake of challenging the unknown? If the early Indo-European conquerors had spent centuries analyzing tables of economic pros and cons, would we ever have had Rome, Sparta, Greek philosophy, the Norse epic or the Vedas?

Bio-engineering will be used to modify humans and perhaps encourage intersexuality and all the LGBTQ crap... what if instead it could eliminate genetic diseases and bring back the original traits of our ancestors, the conquering ones of course, not the ones in monocle bowler hats and walking sticks? And what about the forthcoming discoveries in the quantum and microparticle realms? Having control of matter down to its most basic structure, mastering it to the point of performing wonders that might seem almost magical in the eyes of the masses. "Hu, but so you want to play God...." It is not a game at all, except for the joy that brings with it the will to power of those who feel they are the direct heirs of the great heroes of the sagas and epics of our race who did not see the gods as distant, stern beings who judged those who dared too much but rather the superior beings who welcomed into Olympus or Valhalla the great heroes who went higher and farther. Impassable fences are for herds and flocks, leaving the challenges to others is for slaves. And we want to be wolves and conquerors. Founders of a new era.

# The Operator
# from Ernst Jünger's Total Mobilization
# to Guillaume Faye's Archeofuturism

*Andrea Anselmo*

« When the world falls apart, fissures are created through which are revealed the secrets of architecture that are usually hidden from us ».
Ernst Jünger, *The Adventurous Heart*

Our purpose is to follow up on the interesting discussion Children of Prometheus - The Challenges of Technology and the Future of Humankind.we aired by the web-radio Kulturaeuropa on Saturday June 5th 2021[1].  In particular, we debated the Jüngerian origins of Archaeofuturism, a topic that was proposed to Guillaume Faye himself during an interview in February 2019, shortly before his passing.

It may be of benefit to the reader to recall some of Faye's own best-known statements from his work Archaeofuturism[2]:

« The fallacious idea of progress must be replaced with

---

1        In Italian: *Figli di Prometeo – Le sfide della Tecnica e il futuro dell'Uomo* - Translator's Note (henceforth marked as TN).

2        English edition: *Archeofuturism. European Visions of the Post-Catastrophic Age*, Arktos, 2010.

movement. An astonishing degree of continuity exists between archaic values and the revolutions technological science makes possible. Why? Because the egalitarian and humanitarian mindset of modern man, for instance, does not allow him to manage the explosive possibilities behind genetic engineering or the new electromagnetic weapons [...]. Archeofuturism is a changing worldview. The values of the arché, projected into the future, are made newly relevant and transfigured. The future is not the negation of the tradition and historical memory of a folk, but rather their metamorphosis, by which they are ultimately reinforced and regenerated. To use a metaphor: what does a nuclear-powered ballistic missile submarine have in common with an Athenian trireme? Nothing and everything: one represents the metamorphosis of the other, but both, in different ages, have served precisely the same purpose and embody the same values (including the same aesthetic values). [...] It is necessary to reconcile Evola and Marinetti. [...] It is in the organic, compositional, and radical thought of Friedrich Nietzsche and Martin Heidegger that the new concept of Archaeofuturism is rooted, but structured: thinking together technoscience and the eternal community of traditional society. Never one without the other. [...] The eternal return of the identical versus cyclical and linear visions. Globally, the future demands the return of ancestral values, and this for the whole Earth [...][3] »*

To what extent is Jünger's Arbeiter, who uses technique to mobilize the world, a precursor of that union between Marinetti and Evola that Faye posits as the basis for his Archaeofuturism? How can the mythical dimen-

---

3        The excerpt in *italics* has been translated by me as it does not appear in the English edition and it might be unique to the Italian edition: *Archeofuturismo*, SEB, 1998 (TN).

sion present in the German author - the world of the Titans, the motionless center of movement, the forest - pose itself as a transcendent principle of Archaeofuturism? How can the Jüngerian initiatory path be accomplished through the fire of destruction up to the rebirth of the Arbeiter ruler of technique?

We will attempt to answer these questions in the following pages.

## The Operator, the Outcast and the Anarch

Known to most is the intent of the multifaceted Ernst Jünger to outline, in his literary work, a series of "figures," metaphysical yet immanent categories, in which to some extent the author himself recognized himself and which follow his adventurous life journey. Such a journey starts from his youthful adventures in the Foreign Legion to those with the wanderfoegels; from the trenches of World War I to his work as a national-revolutionary journalist; from passive resistance in Wehrmacht-occupied Paris to the philosophical debate after World War II in Germany.

Actually, his first figure is "implicit," that is, not clearly expressed: it is that of the Krieger, the First World War fighter. The others, however, take on an explicitly theoretical character: the Arbeiter, the Waldganger, and the Anarch.

All three present to some extent translation difficulties, not only from a purely linguistic point of view, but above all from a doctrinal one. A problem not unlike that of the Italian rendering of the language of Martin Heidegger, a friend and admirer of Jünger's work, Der Arbeiter in particular.

The Arbeiter - which we will translate as the Operator, we will see later on what basis we suggest this translation - overcomes the bourgeois order through its different approach with respect to the emergence of the elemental and all that is risky and problematic in the world. Jünger will formulate his well-known maxim "better to be criminal than bourgeois" in the very pages of Arbeiter.

The Arbeiter uses, as already mentioned, technique to mobilize the world; his face gradually mutates into a metallic mask that depersonalizes him but at the same time makes him part of a higher unity, not unlike that of the medieval monastic Orders. Here is a first archeofuturistic trait: precisely in his transcending the bourgeois human type, a moment in which the Operator proves himself capable of surviving the eruption of the elemental, the fire of destruction, the chill of ascetic deprivation (in which the harshness of trench warfare and total mobilization in the field of labor reappear); the hierarchical, sacred and initiatory element of the great monastic-chivalric orders of the Middle Ages reappears. Also because of this sacred, and somewhat alchemical, implication, we prefer the term Operator to Worker or Worker. Even if Jünger wanted in some way to address the national-revolutionary world of Ernst Niekisch and his magazine Widerstand, alliances that would suggest the use of words such as Worker, the latter would not suggest the trait of alchemical transmutation that the term Operator can determine instead. It should be remembered, however, that for Jünger, through danger, risk and the eruption of the elemental the bourgeois human type inevitably disappears.

The Waldganger - which we translate as the Outcast - is the one who goes into hiding. His figure explicitly refers to those who, in medieval Iceland and Germanic society in general, were banished from the community and destined to wander the lands uninhabited by humans. These wastelands were considered to be haunted by disturbing presences: giants, specters and ferocious beasts, which from then on would accompany the outcast, the one who becomes like a wolf to other men.

Jünger's work on the Waldganger, translated in Italy as Trattato del ribelle[4] is easy to find thanks to Adelphi reprints. It pleases Italian readers, mainly because it is considered one of his most innocuous and politically correct writings. In contrast, the text of The Worker/Operator continues to be unread, ignored and sometimes shunned-especially by the many radical chic of various orientations who refer to Jünger. The author himself looks at the earlier figure of the Arbeiter this way:

«With the catastrophes we see figures emerging, which prove themselves equal to the cataclysms and which will outlive them when the incidental names have been long forgotten. Among these figures is, first and foremost, that of the Worker, marching confidently and unswervingly toward its goals. The fires of downfall only serve to throw it into an ever brighter light. For the moment it still radiates an ambiguous titanic glow; we cannot yet guess the royal capitals, the cosmic metropolises in which it will erect its thrones. The world wears its uniform and its armor, and at some point it will also don its festival attire [...]»[5].

Waldganger's suggestions have therefore always had far more space and sympathy among Italian readers than the austere, steelclad propositions of the Worker/Operator. The value of this, as Evola had already recognized, is based first and foremost on the ethical and existential level. But this is not an exclusively "ethical" figure: despite everything, something "metaphysical" moves in the Worker, a figure far more disturbing than the later figure of the "Rebel." Reaching such a metaphysical level, com-

---

4  English edition: *The Forest Passage*, Telos Press Publishing 2013.

5  Ibid., p. 23.

pared to the degradation around us, would be the first step for any serious work of character rectification and the basis, therefore, for genuine asceticism.

Today, therefore, it would be a case of freeing ourselves from the conditioning of bourgeois life and returning to rise on the vertical horizons of the Worker/Operator. A world now inhabited no longer by men, but by consumers and digital users, desperately needs the Worker/Operator who is not the victim but rather the ruler of technology. The rediscovery and deepening of this figure in today's debate tending to ride a-la Evola the archaeo-futurist tiger turns out to be crucial.

We then come to the third Jüngerian figure: the Anarch. The outlander, the underclassman, the straggler, are not authentic translations of the Anarch who differs even from the figure that chronologically precedes him: the Waldganger. The Anarch lends himself very well to being embodied in our everyday reality: he lives in a post-atomic satrapy surrounded by a babel of individuals from all backgrounds but lacking historical destiny; the tyrant who he serves as a bartender is a homosexual, the Condor. But Martin Venator, Jünger's alter ego protagonist, is precisely an Anarch: he uses his job as a bartender to get closer to power and use it to his advantage in his work as a historian. His events are told in Eumeswil, a dystopian novel that anticipates Wikipedia, cell phones and many of the features of our contemporary times. The story of Eumeswil is thus set in a post-apocalyptic future, in a period probably between 2010 and 2020 (curiously, the same temporal setting as Faye's Archeofuturism): the city-state, where "the end of history" is in fact fulfilled, is ruled by a satrapy with an oriental flavor.

The protagonist, Martin Venator, historian by day and bartender to the tyrant in charge of Eumeswil by night, does not, as we have mentioned, live as an outlander or a straggler. He observes power with a keen eye, being an unsuspected dissident thanks to his privileged role at the satrap's side. His name is reminiscent of both the martial and hunting dimensions: a clear reference to Jünger's favorite activities; although in truth by "hunting" the author actually means the work of the entomologist. And it is precisely a great hunting trip that is the event that constantly stands out along the horizon line of the protagonist's events. From the very first pages of the novel, the great hunt in which the entire circle that gathers around the Condor must participate looms as a project but at the same time as an inescapable destiny: references to the wild hunt of the Germanic and Indo-European worlds are probable, as are reminders of the impending Ragnarok, the consummation of the fate of the gods. Such an event, however, is a catastrophe in the etymological sense: a reversal that restores the order of all things, human and divine. In a world, such as that of Eumeswil, in which the end of history has been accomplished, catastrophe thus also implies the regeneration of history itself. The grand and cathartic finale of the novel Eumeswil will coincide with such a great hunt.

« Probably only after catastrophe will have destroyed modernity, with its global myth and ideology, will an alternative view of the world assert itself by virtue of necessity. No one will have the foresight or courage to implement it before chaos breaks loose. It is up to us, therefore, who are living in the interregnum – to use Giorgio Locchi's expression – to develop the idea of the world for the post-catastrophic age. It may be centred on Archeofuturism[6] ».

The implications and affinities of this destiny with

---

6        *Archeofuturism*, op. cit.

the thought of Giorgio Locchi, whose lesson on spherical time is central and basic to Guillaume Faye's archeofuturist formulation, are obvious. But the archaeofuturist aspects in Eumesweil are not limited to the employment of the same philosophical horizon: they also extend to the use of technoscience.

Venator exploits the city-state of the Condor to continue his own historical research using the Luminar, a hypothetical forerunner of Wikipedia created in the catacombs by the mysterious Titans: a computer in which all human knowledge and history has been stored and can be consulted in a kind of virtual reality. Under the guise of a scientific and naturalistic endeavor, Venator explores a series of abandoned bunkers in the wilderness, where he sets up a hiding place for his future "going rogue," to translate the expression "waldgang" in this way. Technoscience, then, becomes the means to pursue archaic and traditional principles, such as the study of history and retreat into the forest.

Thus returns the well-known Jüngerian expression of turning poison into medicine; of using even the most paroxysmal dynamics of contemporaneity to one's own ends and bending them to create spaces of autonomy and freedom.

This is an alchemical perspective along which not only the Jüngerian figures move but also the differentiated man of Julius Evola, whose attitude is admirably described in texts such as Ride the Tiger or The Yoga of Power. On the other hand, here are the terms in which a young Evola expressed himself in his more properly magical period: « A tradition is attested concerning the great work, the creation of a "second Tree of Life." This is the expression used by Cesare della Riviera, in his book The Magical World of the Heroes (Il mondo magico degli

Heroi, 2nd ed. Milan, 1605), where this task is associated with "magic," and generally with the hermetic and magical tradition. Here, the so-called "Left-Hand Path" is of interest. It involves the courage to tear away the veils and masks with which "Apollo" conceals primal reality, transcending forms in order to enter into contact with an elemental world in which good and evil, divine and human, rational and irrational, right and wrong no longer have any meaning. At the same time, it entails knowing how to raise to its peak everything through which the primal terror is exacerbated, and which our natural and instinctive being does not want; knowing how to break through the limit and dig deeper and deeper, inflaming the feeling of a dizzying abyss, and to endure, to persevere in the destructive overcoming that would break other men»[7].

The relationship with the elemental is fundamental to both Jünger's and Evola's initiatory experience: be it the wildfire of the battlefields, the underworld of the Titans, the great Forest that offers refuge, or the wilderness following the great atomic fire that destroys the World State.

## The Jüngerian roots of Archaeofuturism

We have mentioned that the figure of the Jungian Arbeiter foreshadows some of the contents of Archaeofuturism: the ranks of "Operators" with features stiffened into metal masks, forged in the fire of destruction, who constituted a monastic Order capable of using technique to mobilize the world, were a potential prefiguration of the union of Marinetti and Evola proposed by Faye. The figure of the Arbeiter was so seminal that even Evola dedicated a special volume to him, which in many ways al-

---

7        J. Evola, *Dionysus & the "Left-Hand Path"*, translation by G. A. Malvicini, https://juliusevola.wordpress.com/2017/05/27/dionysus-the-left-hand-path/.

ready contains some of the insights for the differentiated man who "rides the tiger."

Genetic engineering, the subject of the new archaeofuturist approach in Faye, also finds a paralell in Jünger's posthumanism, represented by the character of Attila, the doctor in the court of the Condor in Eumeswil. He was an explorer of the Arctic regions of the world, a subtle allusion to that Greenlandic Lay of Atli contained in the Poetic Edda. He, in fact, visited the Hyperborean regions and traversed the great forest that laps the city-state of Eumeswil and to which Venator looks with growing fascination as the final destination of his journey of "hunting" and regeneration, including historical regeneration.

The great Germanic forest is a recurring topos in Jünger's prose, both obviously in Waldgang, as the outcast is the one who is confined to the woods, and precisely in Eumeswil:

«The forest is also a natural dimension. [...] I am very sensitive to the sounds of the forest: the rustling of leaves, the murmur of a stream or the singing of a waterfall. I sense in these musics of nature something that the human word cannot communicate. But apart from that, the forest is for me above all a metaphor: it stands for a virgin territory in which to retreat from civilization now marked by nihilism and in which the individual can still escape the imperatives of the churches and the clutches of Leviathan. In German the words "Heim" home, "Heimat" homeland and "heimlich" secret, have the same root. [...] The forest is secret not only in the sense that it hides, but also in the sense that by hiding, it protects. Strictly speaking, from the Great Loner's point of view, totalitarianism or mass democracy make little difference. The Anarch lives in the interstices of Society, the reality around him is basically indifferent to him, and only when he retreats to his own world, to his own library, does he find his identity. In any case, coolness is recommended: on a frozen swamp one advances with greater confidence and speed. The Anarch hides outwardly in normality; he may be an accountant, carrying out everything that order and law prescribe, but in his inner self, in the solitude of the night, he thinks and does as he pleases. The Anarch fights his own wars even when he marches through the ranks of an army»[8].

Atli also sometimes mentions past laboratory experiments aimed at the creation of new forms of humanity: in other words, the making of the new man.

A prefiguration in the artistic field of the posthuman, consistent with the initiatory and esoteric dimension, is that realized by the artistic work of H.R. Giger, often inspired by the monstrosities of H.P. Lovecraft's universe and in which De Turris himself recognized an alchemical content. Speaking of Giger's Alien, the President of the Evola Foundation in fact expressed himself thus:«Our revulsion, our horror in its presence also stems from the knowledge that it is an essentially ambiguous being: a mixture of natural and unnatural, living and nonliving, human and technological. A symbol of modernity in its uncontrolled technological evolution, perhaps an anticipation of what the Third Millennium holds in store for us»[9].

What could be more inherently archeofuturist than Giger's artistic-alchemical work, where Alien's primordi-

---

8    *L'ultimo Sciamano, conversazioni su Heidegger* ed. by Antonio Gnoli and Franco Volpi, Bompiani 2013. The translation of this excerpt is mine as I could not find an English edition of this essay (TN).

9    *H.P. Lovecraft e H.R. Giger*, ed. by Gianfranco De Turris, in *HRGIGER Visioni di fine millennio*, Hazard Edizioni 1996. The translation of the excerpt is mine (TN).

al ferity derives from Lovecraft's ancient cosmic entities, where the union of bios and technique are magically conjured in the underworld of the mysterious Titans?

Giger defined his monstrosities as biomechanical. Through them he came to illustrate the infamous pseudo-biblium Necronomicon, where bodies, spirits, and machines merge into the same organism.

On the other hand, it is difficult to imagine the post-human without presupposing an intimate relationship between body and spirit: both in the archeofuturist and esoteric sense.

It is no accident that Julius Evola's famous commentary on Ernst Junger's Der Arbeiter addresses the rejection of any rigid dualism between body and spirit: «[The Arbeiter] Is destined to rediscover a great truth that has been lost, namely, that life and worship are one. [...] Therefore any speculative dualism, such as the type [of the Arbeiter] would appear as a kind of heresy or high spiritual betrayal. From dualism - says Jünger -, derive all the antitheses of power and right, of blood and spirit, of idea and matter, of love and sex, of soul and body, of man and nature, of spiritual sword and secular sword, antitheses belonging to a language that will have to be heard as foreign. According to our author [Jünger] these antitheses still feed an endless dialectical discourse, have a corrosive action and eventually lead to nihilism because with them everything is transformed into escapism[10] ».

We think of Ernst Jünger's descriptions of the sculpted bodies of fellow soldiers, which war forged and stripped of unnecessary trappings. We think of the war stories of Pio Filippani Ronconi, where fighting in battle was the outward manifestation of an inner path propitiated by

---

10      *J. Evola, L'operaio nel pensiero di Ernst Jünger, Edizioni Mediter-ranee 1998.* The translation is mine (TN).

appropriate tantric yoga practices, sometimes including paths of magical sexuality.

The themes of eugenics and posthuman engineering are the most extreme culmination of Faye's Archeofuturism: « The incompatibility between modern egalitarian ideology and futurism emerges in the extraordinary limits placed upon the civil nuclear power industry in the West through the influence of manipulated public opinion, or in the pseudo-ethical obstacles raised in opposition to genetic engineering, the creation of 'modified' human beings, and positive eugenics. The more archaic futurism becomes, the more radical it will be; the more futurist archaism becomes, the more radical it will be. [11]». Atli's past experiences, which occurred before the time of the great fires that led to the fall of the world state, constitute his resume "as a doctor at the court of the Condor."

## The initiatory dimension of Jüngerian figures

It seems that it was Jünger himself who described himself as a "mediator of primordial meanings," engaged in delving into authentic "scientific-esoteric" backgrounds where technique, biology and physics would somehow respond to timeless, mythical principles and would be susceptible to their authentically magical-alchemical use. For all these reasons, we find particularly apt the translation of Arbeiter not as Worker, Laborer or Creator but rather as Operator, as one who follows the path of the Ars Regia, Operator in the sense of the Great Work: an alchemical transmutation that determines the overcoming of the bourgeois by means of the synthesis of elements such as the subsoil of the Titans, the metaphysics of immanent figures like the Arbeiter, and technoscience understood as a magical and initiatory form. It is no coin-

---

11      G. Faye, *Archeofuturism*, op. cit.

cidence that Jünger would forge collaborative relations with historian of religions Mircea Eliade and friendship with Argentine writer J.L. Borges, author moreover of a collection of writings entitled The Operator.

« The real is just as fantastical as the fantastical is real [...]. he age has brought home to us the old magical spells which were always present, if long forgotten. We feel that sense begins to weave itself in, hesitantly still, to the great work which we all create, which holds us in its spell»[12].

The esoteric order par excellence in Jünger's literature is that of the mysterious Mauretans: « I have the certainty that a small circle of our people are at work in secret places in the most ancient Tibet », he states in Eumeswil. Atli, explorer and physician devoted to posthumanity, is an old man belonging to the Order of Mauretans. «Wondrous Tibetans, whose monotonous prayers ring out from the cliff-top monasteries of the observatories! Would anyone wish to laugh at prayer wheels who was familiar with our landscapes, with their myriad of revolving wheels — those fierce agitations which move the hour hand of the clock and the furious crankshafts of aeroplanes? Sweet and dangerous opium of velocity! But is it not true that in the innermost centre of the wheel stillness lies hidden? Stillness is the proto-language of velocity. Through translations one would like to see the velocity increase — all these increases can only be a translation of the proto-language. But how is man supposed to understand his own language? »[13].

---

12   E. Jünger, *Sicilian Letter to the Man in the* Moon, translated by A. Faust, https://counter-currents.com/2010/10/ernst-jungers-sicilian-letter-to-the-man-in-the-moon/.

13   Ibid.

# To Die for the West?
# The concept of the Hero in the European world and its demise in the West

*Guido Taietti*

One of the lesser known areas of an already relatively esoteric topic such as Strategy and International Relations is how much the history of a civilization impacts the categories through which that civilization conceives politics and relations with other political actors.

Some speak explicitly of "strategic cultures" to identify precisely the rationalization and optimization of responses to the strategic challenges that a human community has faced in its history, in particular then focusing on the History of the community itself and the geography over which this community has lived and fought. To help the reader let us give a few examples that will make this concept immediately clear and self-evident. Let us consider the concept of retreat in the history of Russian military thought: a retreat is a movement in the opposite direction of the advance, thus a retreat back to one's own lines, which, however, unless it is a rout (thus an unorganized retreat in which troops run to their own back lines in the "every man for himself" manner), does not carry with it any particular emotional drama. A choice that is perfectly acceptable and usable by commanders-in-chief. Needless to specify that in many other military cultures, certainly that of Europe in the past and also in the West today for example, retreat instead is always associated with a moment of suffering and is - at least tactically - a show of defeat or a threat and brings with it for that matter also psychological and reputation costs that must be rectified through war propaganda. Why is retreat instead culturally accepted in the Russian world? Because in the history of the human stock living in the area of Russia, retreat has historically been the way to stretch the opponent's lines, complicate the logistics of the invaders, and lay the groundwork for victory, as it was with Napoleon and Hitler. Anthropologically, Russia is not a densely populated nation and cities tend to be extremely distant from each other so a retreat rarely has an unsustainable human cost; moreover, being the largest nation on the planet, space is literally a no-cost resource for the Russians. But we could give dozens of other examples, we will give just a couple more to show the depth of this approach. China's strategy for example is based on a choice I would define as almost philosophical: not to separate Peace from War as two alternative moments, but to view international relations as inextricably linked to Peace and simultaneously to War. Moments of Peace are moments of low-intensity war or preparation for war; moments of War serve to secure a useful peace. This philosophical-diplomatic premise has heavy strategic consequences, but essentially, they can be summarized by metabolizing the idea that Chinese diplomacy proceeds by not separating political reasoning from commercial or military reasoning. This conception, which is quite alien to us, stems from the fact that historically for centuries Chinese political power had to confront an existential enemy, the Mongol peoples of the North, who having a tribal, clan-based and rarely centralized structure, made developing a system of treaties and agreements very difficult. What is more, such a system would be difficult to maintain due to internal contrasts within the various tribes or among the different clans with whom one could be simultaneously at peace, at war, or in an incomprehensible situation somewhere in-between the two conditions. With this approach, one can understand, for example, why a country that is frequently at war and/or believes it will easily go to war tends not to separate politics from security-related affairs (as is normally the case in Western European democracies): in Israel for example, a country that has experienced more than one war per generation since its birth, the direct consequence of this historical-geographical contingency has meant that there is a strong osmosis between the military, the private sector and politics: finding a politician with a military background is statistically dozens of times easier than finding one in Italy or Germany for example.

**Europe and the concept of the Hero**

The concept of the Hero is typically European, and according to those who espouse this anthropological-strategic approach, this is obviously not accidental. Evidently there must be a historical and geographical reason explaining why the concept of the Hero has become so important and central here. Along with the concept of the Hero, in the European strategic thought there is a set of secondary reflections, such as the idea that retreat is in itself an evil, a condition to be avoided, which obviously act as a corollary to the strategic necessity of creating the concept of the Hero. But what are the conditions that generated the idea of Hero?

For example, the fact that Europe is the densest civilization from the urban point of view: every few kilometers it is possible to find a city, the population is on average very densely distributed, space, from the absolute point of view, is little. Greek civilization was dotted with independent cities among themselves that would certainly unite in case of an external threat but were basically not intertwined in a unified political system of command. Therefore, it was not possible to use retreat as a strategic weapon because to retreat even 40 kilometers, a distance that could be covered in a day by trained men, meant losing perhaps an entire city and its population. In the Italy of World War I, the verses of the best-known song "The Song of Piave" basically illustrate this concept and develop it: "the foreigner does not pass" or it is said that the Italian soldiers "made with their chests a barrier." Why? Because similarly to the Greek context, Italy is an extremely dense space and to retreat 100 km, not an exceptional distance in modern conflicts, means easily losing 2 or 3 medium-sized towns. This is precisely where the idea of Hero has been developed, him being in fact someone who interprets and realizes the good of the community at the cost of personal sacrifice. Not a sacrifice without material benefit, without material results – the Hero rarely responds only to ethics (that would be the Martyr), but usually the Hero achieves a great result and dies in the process of being a Hero. As a Hero of course, he is sanctified and mythicized by the community, transcends his human condition: his mistakes forgiven, his missteps forgotten, he is remembered as a perfect symbol of sacrifice for the national community.

Heroic thinking is in itself anti-utilitarian, at least when seen from the Hero's point of view: he after all agrees to die or sacrifice himself, therefore it is an inherently non-utilitarian thought, although of course "the need for heroes" can safely be considered a rational choice from the point of view of society if one postulates the existence of a mechanism that reasons in collective terms[1].

## The utilitarian West does not like the hero

The West, which was born as an eventuality out of European thought but takes its own trajectory that is both a logical consequence of its origin and at other times totally contradictory to Europe itself, on the other hand, does not like the Hero. Books have been written about how complex it actually is today to distinguish the West from Europe[2], here without going into detail and trusting that everyone can at least separate the two terms in an indicative way, we note that if we consider World War II as the West's attempt to recapture Europe we can at least set 1945 as the purely indicative date when categories pertaining to the West gradually began to eliminate those that pertained to Europe.

Certainly, we can say that the idea of Heroism was one of the first concepts to be targeted, well before ideas that one might expect to be more dangerous to the capitalist West, such as communism, which – from the political and

---

1       We may advance the hypothesis that it is the collective unconscious of a small human community that elaborates this category, but perhaps there are better explanations that we have not yet identified. Marxists, who exactly like liberalists must always postulate reasoning against rational calculation, might believe that the upper classes of society, in order to protect themselves, incentivize the idea of sacrifice on behalf of the community which, as a consequence, also saves their privilege. That may be, but it would seem to me to be an explanation with too many exceptions to stand (many heroes come from the privileged strata themselves for example or many heroes often have political positions that threaten a certain form of privilege, as was, for example, Fascism itself: a phenomenon that stemmed from WWI veterans, based on the rhetoric of the Hero, which in fact was more socialist than the Italian Socialist Party of the time).

2       *A. Scianca, Europa o Occidente, Altaforte 2023.* (Translator's Note: *Europe or the West,* still untranslated in English).

especially cultural points of view - was instead largely tolerated without too much fuss. The idea of the hero, on the other hand, was marginalized, mocked, portrayed as stupid and irrational.

But why such a concentrated offensive to eliminate this concept? Why is it that in Europe today, but in the West in general, the concept of the hero knows no fortune? In my opinion because heroism itself denies the capitalist root that holds up the concept of the West. The capitalist West is based on the idea of individual utility and the rationality of decisions, and of course nothing is more absurd than dying for a cause, that is, to lose the material good *par excellence* that legitimizes the enjoyment of all others (one's own life) in the name of something that does not even potentially offer a material benefit (a "cause").On the contrary, communism was easily accepted because its materialistic premise (aiming at the elimination of material exploitation) is basically totally compatible with the capitalist vision: this was well understood by the Western elites from the late 1970s – when it was clear that the Soviet experiment was faltering under the aspect of economic performance, and this was the real lever that disintegrated the Soviet and communist consensus in the West.

After all, homegrown communists could be asked "Excuse me, but if your worldview is totally materialistic and the Soviet Union today provides living conditions all in all worse for a worker than in the capitalist West, even assuming that a worker here is exploited, why shouldn't he choose the Western model which evidently is so high-performing that even in exploitation it manages to generate so much wealth that the life of the average worker is still better than in the Soviet «socialist paradise"?". The materialistic premise, the lack of a spiritual dimension (reflecting the anthropological similarity between the communist and capitalist-Western visions) was also the reason why, for example, with the collapse of the USSR, communist parties with enormous consensus such as Italy's (which was normally the second most voted party in national elections) collapsed within months: if only the material dimension exists, if something collapses or fails it has in failure the very explanation of its own irrationality. This view is alien to, for example, fascism, which was always essentially an anti-materialist and therefore anti-capitalist movement. This is why in fact the collapse of fascism and its demonization after the defeat of World War II, unlike the communist case, did not mean that the model had failed or that it was necessary to automatically abandon the cause, so much so that fascism maintained a degree of consensus in Italy for a time (and it still does).

The Hero therefore, being anti-materialistic, anti-individualistic is in itself anthropologically anti-Western and anti-capitalistic. On the other hand, one should not think that there was only an ideal or anthropological motivation for eliminating the idea of the hero: there was also a brutally strategic one. The West owes its military supremacy basically to its economic, logistical and quantitative advantage. Therefore, the project of eliminating the idea of the hero, the idea of a sacrifice taken to the extreme, the idea of the acceptance of the irrational, is quite understandable because if potential competitors agree to confront each other on the level of material means, avoiding heroism or overly irrational attitudes the West can only win. Conceiving war as a stock market, an infinite set of rational exchanges where no other evaluations than economic ones intervene, can only benefit those who start with a superior material condition: a bit like playing poker with someone with a much larger amount of money than you, playing endless games and all as mathematically sensible as possible, would essentially end (having brought the weight of all other variables to zero) with the victory of those who start with a more substantial budget. Indeed, even if one accepts the idea, on the theoretically perfectly rational level, that there is no point in waging a war that cannot be won, theoretically the West, always enjoying the large initial quantitative advantage, could trust that all other actors would always basically give in to its demands knowing that, in any case, the war could only be lost.

But of course, reality is different: and not because this process of reification of the real has not yet been completed and not all civilizations accept to consider the exclusively material plane and/or reject the irrationality of war altogether. At this point, however, it is up to ourselves, who as Europeans or descendants of Europeans (which then is, racially speaking, almost the same thing) should ask ourselves whether we in our turn, while living the schizophrenic condition of Westerners AND Europeans, should not at least work to recover the idea of the Hero; if in turn we may still have some ground to cover before even beginning to discuss political struggle. In my opinion, the answer is *yes* and the first step is to recover a sacred, anti-economist dimension of life, to recover the idea of the Hero. The communists believed that the alternative to usury and to the market was debate and they not only lost, but proved to be the best allies for an evolved form of capitalism so disinterested in the future of peoples and ethnicities that we are left to wonder if there is an agenda that actively aims at mixing them. We, on the other hand, quoting Pound, know that the alternative to the market is not debate, but the Temple, the idea of the Sacred, the transcendent.

"The Temple is holy because it is not for sale."

# Interstellar imperative

*Francesco Boco*

Mankind has always scanned the depths of the starry sky in search of answers to its questions. Is this fragile and ingenious life form the only one in the universe, or are there other inhabited planets? Will other life forms be able to challenge man's role tomorrow? In recent years, a feverish search for habitable planets with atmospheres similar to Earth's has intensified these questions, which are still clearly unanswered. This impulse is driven by a sense that the exploitation of the biosphere will lead to an unsustainable situation for all terrestrial life forms unless the space and resources to support human development are found elsewhere. Space telescopes are attempting to detect some Earth-like planets in the relatively close (four light-years) Alpha Centauri and Proxima Centauri systems. Meanwhile, space agencies such as Nasa and SpaceX have long turned their studies to the possible colonization of Mars or the Moon. According to experts, they foreshadow the possibility of an interplanetary civilization, which will require substantial investment and a very long time to realize. The desert of Mars, according to some, could be transformed into a land where we could find essential resources for the survival of the human species.

However, leaving Earth's magnetic field and the long duration of the journey to the Red Planet are two aspects that affect exploration missions. Astronauts are exposed to radiation that can cause vision and memory loss, while the absence of gravity can cause bone degeneration and organ failure. In short, the exciting aspects are countered by a number of issues that must be carefully addressed if the Mars mission is to bear fruit and be the beginning of a terraforming process, that is, the creation of conditions for human life. It is thought that the first human landing on Mars, followed by a return after six or seven months, could take place in 2030 or, more likely, around 2040.[1]. Humans will have to develop suitable equipment for planetary survival, and aerospace technology will have to be able to bring them back by employing reusable rockets.

There are many complications, but since the 1970s Western science has been studying the issue of interstellar exploration and expansion. Obviously, it will be an issue of great importance to future civilizations. The outcome depends entirely on how this issue is addressed. The series of legitimate questions raised by the prospect of human expansion into space, such as whether the purpose is exploitation or sharing, or whether it is based on cooperation or corporatism, run up against a fundamental assumption that could be the weakness of such a major long-term project. Interstellar exploration and the associated appropriation of new habitats is indeed an increasingly urgent imperative, assuming that the level of technoscientific development and the associated exploitation

---

1       *See National Geographic, n. 5, novembre 2016, Milan (Italian Edition).*

of Earth's resources are to be maintained, increased, and expanded. In fact, there are two main factors: population growth and the depletion of raw materials needed for energy production. To these two factors must be added a third, which concerns the possibility of environmental disasters caused by technological development that is not ecologically sustainable for the planet. This is obviously the intention, encouraged by the Western humanitarian and universal vision, to promote and foster development also in all the so-called Third World countries. This would entail a gradual retreat from agriculture in favor of urbanization, which would inevitably be followed by an increase in emissions, pollution, overpopulation, and other factors causing social and political instability. If these are concrete reasons for directing the efforts of human beings outside their cradle, on the other hand, it is the case to note that precisely technoscientific development is a determining factor of civilization, specifically located and determining the possibilities in terms of expansion, production, exploitation and environmental protection of individual states and nations. It may be that an uncontrolled development of the entire human race and its total access to primary resources may cause a sudden collapse of precisely that civilization of technology that is believed to be the only one that can guarantee forward momentum for its own protection. Not only common sense should prompt a reconsideration of the global technological race, but also a more forthright approach to the technoscientific knowledge on which the possibilities of the future are based. For it is clear that the scientific knowledge essential for galactic exploration is not commonly accessible and widely disseminated; even less so are the necessary means and funding for space missions. Possession of the knowledge and means is a non-random factor that is bound to affect the possibilities of terraforming in the long run. Said explicitly: those who possess the knowledge, tools and funds will decide the ways, times and purposes of this process of allowing human beings to spread beyond their home planet. Up until now, the strong argument in favor of interstellar missions is the desire to secure a future for human civilization. A phrase that in its noble and universalist tone hides a profound contradiction that risks sinking an incredibly ambitious project. This internal contradiction is primarily the result of an overconfidence in the intentions of the elites promoting galactic expansion on the one hand, and on the other hand of a naive belief in the existence of a fraternal humanity united by common values and common feelings. The first aspect depends on the fact that interstellar missions respond first and foremost to political interests and certainly not to humanitarian purposes. On the other hand, it is difficult to think of a human civilization credibly and substantially characterized by shared values and equal expectations. After all, it is not the scientists and engineers who decide on the purpose of space missions but the elites who finance, design and oversee those same missions. There are those who have spoken of post-biological societies, i.e., those in which the biological imperatives that would characterize cohesive civilizations would become less important due to the emergence of a kind of post-humanity that is no longer dependent on biological limits: neural chips, longevity extension, sensory spectrum amplifiers, genetic engineering, etc., would place the ability to shape life entirely in the hands of humans, leaving only a small role for "nature". The development and application of these technologies would, on the one hand, create favorable conditions for space colonization and, on the other hand, mark even more sharply the differences between humans and civilizations, dividing them according to access to technologies, scientific skills, and the degree of complexity achieved.[2].

Here, then, to speak of a human civilization to be protected is at the very least imprecise and vague, in a context that instead demands the utmost precision and rigor. Some use the term "interstellar civilization," and perhaps behind this lies a glimpse of a Western sunset, an attempt to escape from shortcomings that cannot and will not be corrected. One can certainly assume that a new postbiological "human type" will emerge from the experience of the extreme frontier, but at the very least one must consider who will really be the primogenitor of this crossing of the threshold of humanity, and what will be the minimum homogeneous characteristics of the inhabitants of the emerging space civilization. On the one hand, we are dealing with people with high IQs, extraordinary physical abilities, and a strong super-cultural adaptability to new living conditions; people who have been thrown into a completely artificial creative process. We are standing at a threshold that is at once anthropological and ontological, which calls upon the connective structure that binds all human beings in their unique peculiarities. Identity is a determination that is subject to change and tension when confronted with what is different from ourselves, but symbolic memory always retains a decisive importance that cannot be erased or evaded. The extreme case of encounters of opposites is an intrinsic aspect of civilization, in the sense that maximum tension is found when two opposite ontological determinations come into contact. This is the case of so-called hot and cold civiliza-

---

2       *L'orizzonte postumano e la civilizzazione interstellare, 6 giugno 2008, online:* www.fantascienza.com. *(Translator's Note: The Posthuman Horizon and Interstellar Civilization, 6 June 2008, untranslated in English).*

tions. The former are those that are historically operative, at the forefront of a Faustian process of technical and cognitive conquest; the latter are mainly those that are tribal or otherwise petrified in a backward stage of cultural development - not according to Western parameters, but from their own specific original datum of hominy. As Giorgio Locchi has rightly pointed out[3], these cold, i.e., a-historical, societies, by their refusal to go further betray the primal act of the founder. The non-random encounter between men belonging to warm, i.e., historical, civilizations and "cold" men inevitably calls the latter into question, placing them in tension with themselves in the first place. The unknown calls into question the ontological choice that holds the group of men together, because it can be either a mortal threat or a creative opportunity. That is, it is a choice between a passive and an active attitude, between two different conceptions of the human. More radically and decisively, interstellar exploration is an internal fact of techno-scientific civilization, but one that has nothing to do with a supposed unity of purpose of borderless peoples, since it takes on the characteristics of a contest for scientific primacy among particular cultures and world views. What makes us question humanity - tomorrow and perhaps even today - is not only the unknown, but it is actually the historical man who calls himself to stand before an epochal decision that marks a decisive moment in the path of future civilizations, like a

---

3        *«An authentic human science can only establish itself with a humane definition of man, recognizing in historicity the property of human reality. Consequently, its field of experience and of verification can be found only in history: history gone by, and history to come», G. Locchi, Etology and the Human Sciences, translated by F. Cullen and published online: https:// www.academia.edu/43723872/Giorgio_Locchi_Ethology_and_the_Human_ Sciences_1979. Originally in Italian as Etologia e scienze umane in G. Locchi, Definizioni, Milano 2006, p. 66.*

new Neolithic. This opening of time would not be possible if we had reached the "end of history".

Since the Westernization of the world is not yet complete, and a number of identities persist to varying degrees, terraforming projects will certainly not be an extension of the identical, but could be an evolution, improvement, and extension of the origin of a given civilization. So what is a civilization? A civilization is a complex, territorially located cultural aggregation that is distinguished from the outside world by anthropological, cultural, legal, etc. characteristics. Civilization is the determination of an ontological choice that goes back to a living and shared primordial belonging. Therefore, it is understood that space exploration is certainly a new frontier of civilization, but *for each* of those who will engage in this mission of momentous importance. Indeed, it is not within the reach of all peoples and cultures of the world to design and envision processes of terraforming and transhumanization, but these are possibilities that require first of all a solid ontological foundation and a very strong historical tension. By ontological foundation we mean the core of Being on which all authentic civilizations rest. Martin Heidegger argued that the human being is authentically realized only when he grasps himself entirely in his historical limitation. Through the realization of being a being-towards-death, humans can understand the authentic dimension of their destiny. By anticipating himself through decision, man overcomes its limitedness and stands on a plane of authenticity that participates in the original Being. For Heidegger, the origin is the core that always remains hidden but can always be drawn upon. In the moment he foresees his death, man can then lower himself historically as a participant in his own specific Being. In this sense, a dying civilization, that is, the human fact of long duration *par excellence,* which stands before its extreme possibility, can set a different course for history by taking up the challenge with a decision of ontological scope. This means that a civilization, any civilization, placed before the very real possibility of disappearing and exhausting itself, can find the strength to re-found and regenerate itself by relocating itself in its origin and placing the origin before itself as a project.

It is likely that when interstellar missions will have borne lasting fruits and initiate concrete possibilities for the colonization of other planets, variations of the home civilization characterized by strong cultural homogeneity and a very high cognitive level will originate. This will create the conditions for a renewal of each civilization according to their distinctive characters. But for this to happen, it is indispensable that philosophy provide the foundations of a thought open to epochal challenges and not held back by moralism and reassuring eschatological narratives. As Guillaume Faye argues[4], the best reaction to such a challenge is to find archaic answers to futuristic problems.

It is possible that in at least one part of the world, civilizational specificities will come back strongly, in the wake of the general awakening of biodiversity. This will affect the approach to the future and the potential provided by technologies. Each civilization will decline technological development in its own way and to its own advantage, and it is therefore conceivable that, starting from these assumptions, in the first place any human civilization scientifically up to the mark will aim at prolonging itself, that is, laying the foundations on minimum parameters of cultural homogeneity from which to start. The devel-

---

4  G. Faye, *Archeofuturism. European Visions of the Post-Catastrophic Age, Arktos, 2010..*

opments of such a situation, considering that human beings will not necessarily be satisfied with reaching a satisfactory end point but will tend to set themselves new goals all the time, fall, at the moment, within the vast realm of hypotheses. Aeneas left Troy as it was burning, guided by auspices that led him to the land of the Latins where, they said, he would found a city destined to rule peoples. Deep within European culture there is this epic and courageous origin, which drives one to prolong one's civilization even under the most extreme conditions. In Lucretius as in Heraclitus, becoming takes on the characters of an unceasing challenge in which man descends as a factor of balance and imbalance, called to an effort to understand and act that is ultimately capable of harnessing energy, directing it and at the same time exalting its mystery and power. This cultural, rational and objective origin speaks through etymology but also in the operation that reactualizes the archaic ritual by continuously updating its configurations according to the historical context. Being, as Heidegger puts it, becomes history and it is the product of a civilization authentically placed in the origin that constantly renews and regenerates itself.

# Reclaiming the Torch of Technology: Thinking Revolution in the Time of the Infosphere

*Guido Taietti*

Though the process is still ongoing, the inversion between the real and the virtual is a fact, even for the common man: the centrality of the world is now on the virtual plane while what happens outside, but fails to access the virtual, is at best residual. The increased ability to generate surplus value on the virtual plane, the greater technical advancements achieved, the social diffusion of technology and the emergence of the first generations who live almost entirely "online" are the main factors that have contributed to generating this reversal. This process also has interesting consequences for the way reality is conceived by the great mass of human beings who approach historical phenomena (of which technological evolution and the fusion of technology and politics is but a part) in an essentially passive way: reality is told to the great mass of human beings by the possessors of technology or at least by those who manage to govern the narrative process by disentangling themselves from the algorithms, the boundaries and the ability to control them placed by the possessors of technology; the public, on the other hand, reworks this narrative as little as possible, largely on the basis of what they can understand and merely they attach to it the information they already have. What is real, for the story user, is today only hyper-real[1] or a dis-homogenous sum of hyper-realities: a microscopic, partial event that occurred on the planet, but amplified and viralized by the infosphere becomes "reality," "the story." A huge, massive event with blood and death, if marginalized and relegated by the infosphere, becomes "an anecdote". The process of socialization itself [2] is little by little being subsumed by the virtual, and every social experience today is mediated by the virtual, which, however, being at the moment not a neutral or merely "technical" ground, but an owned and political one, interferes with that process according to its own logic and agenda. Therefore, for the man-mass, the object of historical phenomena, every social process loses its autonomy and becomes mediated, if not directly governed, by the apex, by those who own the social infrastructure. Friendship, for example, today evolves through online acquaintance or on social networks, but on these platforms some topics are banned, some authors are banned, and some ideas are marginalized or, worse, are spread in a partial way[3]. But a similar argumentation

1       *According to Baudrillard's fortunate definition: the hyper-real is reality told by the media, a reality that is disassembled, segmented, picked out, parceled out, reassembled, fictionalized but ultimately, precisely because it is fake it is more interesting and ultimately more "real" than reality for the audience.*

2       *Socialization is the process of internalizing moral categories and values that occurs throughout an individual's life by precisely encountering various social entities, the family first (primary socialization), but also at school, in the peer group or through friendships (secondary socialization).*

3       *In fact, the form of censorship that works par excellence is not that which makes ideas or authors unavailable, a problem that could be solved by looking for answers elsewhere, but that which provides a partial or wrong answer to the question because by satisfying the need to search it still returns*

could be made about the process of falling in love, the enjoyment of cultural goods such as music, videos, etc. There is almost no possibility for human beings to access their "social" side without being filtered by info-Corporations that can manipulate this process by directing it, eliminating certain words, ideas, outputs or by simply monitoring it. This socialization process, in the past and even today, has historically been a complex and segmented one: an individual would learn the different facets of society and social values by encountering different segments of society and different views of it: in the family, at school, reading newspapers, with friends, etc.: nowadays most of these processes (excluding perhaps the relationship with close family members, and I suspect this is one of the reasons why the idea of the family is despised by the woke-corporations) are mediated by the network, which ceased to be free long ago and is basically the manifestation of the political and social agenda of a handful of corporations.

As technology will allow it (actually it already allows it, it is society rather that is slow to adapt to the rhythms of technology) the whole social development, every social exchange, will be mediated by technology. Whereas the value system of an individual of the last generation was built in the meeting-collision of the information a human being could come across at school, in the family, among friends, in a party branch, at the stadium, in books, within the next generation all these agents of socialization will be replaced by a supposedly theoretical plethora of new agents, all of them virtual and therefore all responding roughly to a single political and ideological agenda. We can call this more or less theoretical point as "social singularity." A process in which almost all of the

_______________

*a biased result to those who were at least trying to search for information.*

information accessible to an individual has to go through the network and then through the private or state agents who control the network turning the network into a kind of huge instrument of human domestication. It goes without saying that this inherently undesirable process – especially since the owners of technology at the moment do not have a particularly favorable view of the White Man and his mission – is nevertheless a fundamentally inescapable process with which we must somehow come to terms. Rather, the big question is "how to confront this process?" rather than questioning whether or not this meeting-clash is appropriate. While Luddite, "disconnective" solutions may have some individual functionality they are politically harmful because it is unthinkable for a human community endowed (or wishing to endow itself) with destiny to consider disconnecting from the virtual as a solution unless we want to end up like the native Amerindians when the Spanish arrived in the 16th century. Instead, to begin with, it is at the very least necessary to re-politicize the very concept of Technique (i.e., to bring back it to the center of a collective reflection concerning the Community as a whole and its interests).The idea that technique is a neutral effect, almost parallel to human history, a kind of independent variable against which one can place oneself only exceptionally as a technician or as a user, fosters that passive attitude in the face of technique that benefits the current "masters". It is a fact, of course, that at present those who own the technique are human types substantially opposed to the heroic vision to which we refer and even more so to the white man himself, but on closer inspection we could make the same argument when speaking of politics or economics, and likewise we would find it unreasonable to suggest apolitical attitudes or disinterest in economics.

Likewise, we need to re-appropriate technical thinking and construct categories and pathways to counter and confront the process of "social singularity" not by shunning it, but by opposing other processes that are mobilizing and affirming. The very idea of "Political Witchcraft"[4], issue that we have addressed elsewhere, however, basically fits into this reasoning: "how can radical political actors communicate effectively if the context in which communication takes place is no longer a neutral infrastructure, but a platform with its own agenda contrary to the one belonging to radical actors?" We have proposed both technical and theoretical ideas, but of course that is not the point: technical solutions will be overtaken by events probably in an unreasonably short time, what is important, however, is to state a theoretical principle: this process exists and is neither neutral nor should it be passively embraced as if we were users. On the contrary, it is necessary to re-politicize it, to orient it as far as possible, to build more of it, to improve it. The solution is not to be subjected to History and Technology, the solution is to be their Active Masters.

We need to leave the moralistic approach that says we are right as we are good even if we are losing, and we need to reclaim a more Nietzschean approach (or Greek too) according to which we "would be even *better* if we won".

Because this is first of all a clash of powers, of the forces behind a worldview, and first of all one must understand that the force behind the ideas themselves is, fortunately or unfortunately, more important than the ideas themselves. Nietzsche said "the politician sees

---

4        G. Taietti, *Stregoneria Politica: Manuale di comunicazione politica non convenzionale*, Altaforte 2021. *(TN: Political Witchcraft: A Manual of non-conventional political communication, still untranslated in English).*

human beings as obstacles or as instruments," and all in all, Capital, in protecting itself, in its own reifying process in which everything is devoured, parceled out and valorized, is carrying out a political process. The problem possibly is whether those who oppose it – in addition to doing so on an ideal, abstract level, of pure talk perhaps even as an end in itself and thus all in all nothing more than passively conservative – know how to do the same. They need to build mechanisms and identify contrary or alternative historical processes to be adhered to, empowered, directed and they even need to know how to anticipate, create new ones or at least be in the right place at the right time. Because political reflections, if they stay so and do not somehow precipitate to have consequences on the level of Technique, on the level of Economics, on the level of "how it is done" in addition to the question of "what is done," are in danger of being little by little marginalized, censored, reduced by powers they do not know to being almost more provocative literature. In any case, the reflection is first and foremost conceptual: "how to position oneself towards Technique," or even better, " how to position oneself towards Technique in order to achieve a certain end" - and out of this reflection a certain degree of responses can emerge, and even if they are only tactical, they are nonetheless usable. The use of social media, for example, until about 2018 was a phenomenal tool in the hands of the most radical political realities in the West, which, by communicating much better than the more mainstream and congealed political actors, enjoyed for a time a great deal of leverage to achieve greater visibility. Little by little, over the years, platforms have increasingly implemented a more active and political management of their content and now instead doing radical politics on social networks tends to be much more complex; however, once one understands what is happening and why it is happening, it is always possible to work out a solution: some messages get through on social networks anyway, or one alternates the use of the different platforms in the social ecosystem according to one's needs, or one invents alternative methods of communication such as memes that are often too quick or too cryptic to be effectively censored. And so images and cartoons, initially emerging almost as a waste product from the social ecosystem, have become tools for disseminating political messages. They became, at least for a time, "perfect bullets", a minimal communicative unit capable of uniting a face, a situation with an emotion, a laugh, a message, a slogan. Probably in a reasonably short time even memes will be anesthetized by the platform owners who, as owners, have both the tools to see their use and the resources to proceed to limit the phenomenon, perhaps with the use of AI refined enough to catch double entendres and sarcasm. The point however stays the same: memes became a political weapon and worked for a time because, consciously or unconsciously, active minorities were able to make political use of it. In a context of almost total disadvantage it has been a powerful tool of cognitive warfare (on the other hand in NATO circles memes have also been referred to as the "IEDs of the infosphere") and are a good case study of how one has to actively approach Technique in order not to be completely crushed by it (though this has been, all in all, a tactical and limited response compared to the size of Technique itself of course). It is relevant, therefore, that regardless whether it is Technique that shapes the world (as argued by both some accelerationists and actually some Luddites such as the well-known Ted Kaczynski), or whether it is Politics, ideas, and qualified minorities that shape the world and thus also direct Technique toward some shores rather than others, it remains that it is not possible not to confront it, not only and perhaps not so much on the theoretical level as on the factual level. The increased ability to handle information, the tendency to extract value from the real by mathematizing it, the attempt to control and demobilize or destroy political minorities that may be opponents of the current ruling classes and the values they advocate are phenomena that have always existed and that we simply perceive today as "quantitatively" different, but they will not cease to exist because they have always existed and are intrinsically present in the very concept of Politics, they occupy perhaps its interstices or shadowy areas but they have always existed and will not cease to exist. Therefore, it is a priority that every active minority, every potential new ruling class (for this is, sociologically, a revolution: the rapid replacement of a ruling class and their values with another carrying a different worldview) should ask itself what categories to use to move within the Technical universe, just as it is expected to have new and proper categories to move within the Political, Economic and Social universe.

# A multidimensional view of technique

*Francesco Boco*

According to the leading representatives of the accelerationist current of thought, technology is a means by which chaotic forces, deeply hidden in the earth's crust, make their way toward a total takeover of existence. This takeover results in the questioning of the primacy of man, who is ultimately forced to confront and abdicate to annihilating powers with alien characteristics. The domination of global capitalism, in its financial, political or military declinations, is realized in a nihilistic movement of leveling and equalization.

On a closer inspection it can be argued that globalism, that is, the financial and commercial exploitation of the entire planet Earth, aims at reaching a ground zero of sorts, a simplification of existence such that any aspect of life at any latitude can be brought back into the meshes of the system.

The victory of the unique global model would thus be accomplished, shaping a world where relevant differences are no more and they suit perfectly the survival of the capitalist mechanism.

## Accelerationism: the self-understanding of the system

The possibility to conceive – even if only theoretically – a unified world, deterministically bent on an *inevitable* end has much in common with the monotheistic interpretation of history. Whether the Promised Land is a concrete place or a spiritual one, it matters little. What matters is that there is an end point, and event that will put an end to suffering and enable believers to break free once and for all of the yoke of becoming, decay and oblivion. This can be achieved only by going, gradually, all-out scorched-earth. By annihilating identities, resetting strong affiliations to zero. By any means and by any deception. A necessary trauma to achieve greater goals. The destruction of heresy.

The majority of accelerationists show that they belong, both inwardly and in practice, to the monotheistic thought pattern, which makes them believe in the inevitability of the capitalist model, its absolute and lasting hegemony and the practical impossibility of realizing an alternative to this system. This being the case, it cannot be brought down with a revolution, but at most traversed until reaching a point of saturation, when nothing historically relevant will happen again[1].

A unified world under *one* God. One people governed by *one* universal law. The seething of entities unleashed with the intent to put to good use the nihilistic chaos into which society sinks and eventually consumes itself. The nihilistic chaos we refer to here is the core from which technologies draw, the frightening energies that run through the nervous system of the world. Their control is only momentary. The dissolving process takes place in

---

1     See N. Land, *Collasso*, Rome 2020 (Translator's Note: a collection of Nick Land's writings translated into Italian and published by Luiss Press); B. C. Han, *Capitalism and the Death Drive*, Cambridge 2021.

the wake of a self-fulfilling messianic prophecy. Finally, man will have to yield and, in a Hegelian fashion, make way for the spirit of the age and the victory of the new over the old. Monotheism results in uniformity, one-dimensionality - the favored hunting ground for predatory potentates whose primary goal is to nullify existence. The realization of an overarching system is the only possible outcome; it must be unquestionable and essentially irreplaceable.

This inevitability of the system has much of the monotheistic determinism, founded on the linear, thus fragmented and finalistic, view of historical time and on a rigid moralistic dualism, which divides the members of the community of the faithful from their enemies. A determinism politically declined for other things according to the principle of *necessity*: the necessary social structure, the best of all possible worlds. Achieved, however, according to accelerationism, at the price of the annihilation of man as such, sacrificed to alien and brutal deities. There is no superhumanity in sight. Accelerationism has at least two formal flaws that deeply mark its hermeneutics of the technical *reality*: its insistence on monotheistic Judeo-Christian thought and linguistic patterns and the belief that, ultimately, the principle that originates from and governs technique is something alien, something foreign to the human essence.

## Organizing complexity

Accelerationist discourse usually is punctuated by esoteric references of various kinds, but hardly ever does hermeneutic research turn to ancient Indo-European languages: Greek, Latin or Old Germanic. This means that these authors' horizon of meaning is marked by a distinct cultural choice, which conditions their worldview.

The mindset one derives from, for example, linking one's reading of the present and the future to the Kabbalah, Islamic esotericism, or Middle Eastern demonology [2] is certainly different from the one obtained by reactivating a connection with Greek or Nordic myths in the interpretation of planetary technology. It is therefore not surprising that for all accelerationists, from Nick Land to Mark Fisher, the techno-capitalist set-up is not in question and is considered the only possible system. One God, one system. Whether this then takes on the features of a confused pseudo-religious esotericism is of no interest here.

Therefore, if one wants to find the interpretive key to be able to think of a viable alternative to the current system, one must necessarily break out of its mental patterns, that is, try to free thought and language from the ballast that prevents one from broadening the horizon and expanding historical perspectives. For if one moves in the rut of an already established inevitability, any genuine historical free will shall find itself incapable of producing effect. Things are fortunately more complex, and the unexpected often pops up in the course of events to remind us that the last word has not been spoken yet. In a nutshell: any vision that advocates any declination of the "end of history" is profoundly anti-European[3].

Europe's inability to make itself an active power in the field of global technology is probably conditioned by worldviews and mental cages that restrain its real possibilities. In the present condition, it is impossible to draw on the true European origin to derive the answers and orientations to the present and future challenges; the future indeed appears hazy, confusing and incomprehen-

---

2       See: R. Negarestani, *Cyclonopedia*, Melbourne 2008.

3       See: G. Locchi, *Sul senso della storia*, Padova 2016 (TN: *On the meaning of history*, still untranslated in English).

sible. But it is often radical action that thins out the uncertainties and charts paths that previously could not be discerned. What is required today is an act of strength, a decisive will, which is oriented by a thought that is as authentically European as possible, hence original. According to such philosophical dystopias, technology can be generically interpreted as a means of dehumanization with a will of its own. Beyond the more or less fanciful interpretations, there are no Terminator-style "revolts of the machines" in sight today and for the next few years: every technical product depends on its creator and programmer, it does not have a will of its own nor can it acquire it. At most, as in the case of AI, it can combine human-provided information to learn behaviors, but always from a wealth of experience produced and collected by humans. If man could really be replaced by AI, this would depend on a vacuum left by a man who has fallen into the dimension of inauthenticity, lost in the formless multitude, and it would not be due to the alleged danger posed by machines. A man who abdicates his role, his inventive power and spirit of adventure, deserves to be replaced by stronger and braver creatures[4].

## The furrows of memory

The Mannaz rune at this point provides some interpretive insights. It is connected to Mannus, son of the Germanic god Tuisto, divine ancestor of the first three Germanic tribes, similar to Romulus and Aeneas. The name of the rune comes from the Proto-Germanic *mann-*, which is derived from the Proto-Indo-European *mon-* and *men-*. The former means man, warrior, virile; the latter, *men-*, adds the dimension of thought. It has to do

---

4        See: Vv. Aa. *Prometheica*, vol. 5, Milano 2023 (TN: still untranslated in English).

with memory and its preservation, with repeating and passing on, even to the point of being correlated with foretelling and vaticination. The Mannaz rune is also a communal rune, that is, it alludes to the family and tribal dimension, where the preservation and continuity of tradition and lineage are effectively accomplished[5]. Mimir, one of the oldest Norse giants, is keeper of memory, bringer of knowledge and adviser to Odin, to whom he reveals secret wisdoms. Mannaz then represents the initiatory journey to the origin and the "augmented" return, that is never the same. It symbolizes memory that draws on primordial knowledge, collects it and orders it into ever new forms. It is a process like the one of the initiate/*magician*. Memory can therefore be considered a deep well/*server* from which the mind/*artificial intelligence* draws what it needs with ever-changing outcomes, creating small or big modifications in the world around it. Much depends on *which* memory one chooses to activate.

Even a cursory examination of the Indo-European peoples reveals communities that were able to create and use technical tools without restraint. The Romans, for example, were exceptional designers and builders of rationally organized cities centered on spiritual centers (the temples). What made Roman engineering so effective was probably the *forma mentis* imparted by an education based on logical thinking, on a clear rationalization of words and meanings. Anyone who has studied Latin knows how precise but clear and consistent the grammatical rules were. Through this organization of language and thought, it is possible to achieve extraordinary technical results. Similarly, law and the organization of justice are among the most significant technical facts of the

---

5        Cfr. F. Perizzolo, *Rune. Sacro e identità*, Florence 2023, p. 79 (TN: *Runes. The Sacred and Identity*, still untranslated into English).

Roman world.

On the other hand, it is no coincidence that Athena was the most important goddess to the Greeks. Daughter of Zeus, synonymous with wisdom, goddess of the arts and justice, she represented a sublimated form of reason, much more akin to intuition than to modern rationality. Even in this illustrious case, we show that rational, creative thought had its own important role in the Indo-European world, but that it emerged from a multidimensional, dynamic, and spatially situated ontology. Each deity was embedded in a plural and rooted set of divinities, that is, meanings and active faculties. The mistake made at least from the Enlightenment onward consisted in seeking the one God in Reason and thus conferring on it all the trappings of the immobile center of everything. It is no wonder that this supposed uniqueness of Enlightenment reason was later reversed into its apparent chaotic and dehumanizing opposite. Absolutes tend, after all, to twist themselves into their own extreme opposite.

## Beyond reason

Reason initiates man into a potentially unlimited dominion over the world. The power of the individual, through the cost-benefit rationale, soon moves to another level, that of man's dominion over man. Here the modus dominandi is expressed in all its power. If domination over nature, over the world, was a matter of ordering and gathering its hidden powers for the benefit of human existence, the domination of reason over man becomes a functional, bureaucratic power. Finally, in its path of self-justification, reason imposes its unquestioned yoke on men and things against any free criticism. Reason absolutizes itself as a method of organizing the planetary totality, to which one must submit without being able to criticize it. What was supposed to be an emancipatory force from the dark irrationality of the divine or the mythical norm, in turn takes on the characteristics of something sacred, unquestionable. This happens because reason is self-justifying, it is not based on anything superior or prior, it is the founding principle of itself, and in this spiral of thought lies the fundamental risk of neutralizing any real power of thought.

In short, the Enlightenment traces a theoretical path through which it turns into what it set out to deny, because the application of reason acquires an unlimited potentiality that frees it from Kantian optimistic limits and places it on a plane of autonomy, so that it objectifies the subject in its work of nullification. It is finally made explicit as a use of the will to power. The subject-object logic, on which all modern rationality is based, enters into a contradiction and an ontological crisis that forces us to look at the limits of thought in the face of the unlimited power of reason: « By sacrificing thought, which in its reined form as mathematics, machinery, organization, avenges itself on a humanity forgetful of it, enlightenment forfeited its own realization By subjecting everything particular to its discipline, it left the uncomprehended whole free to rebound as mastery over things against the life and consciousness of human beings »[6].

Nick Land has cryptically and dystopically described the drift to which reason-driven progress leads. If the Kantian intention is to place limits on the subject, it soon becomes clear that what remains unthinking and dissolving outside arbitrarily placed limits is by no means deprived of power or excluded from technical discourse. On the contrary, the moment rationality enters into the

---

6  M. Horkheimer – T. W. Adorno, *Dialectic of* Enlightenment, Stanford 2002, p. 33.

mechanical, statistical and economic organization of the globe, forces come into play that follow their own rationality, in which man himself is held and exploited. At this point, man loses his ontological stature; he is reabsorbed as a function of an artificial process that invests everything, including life. «Machine desire may seem inhuman because it tears apart political cultures, erases traditions, dissolves subjectivities, and hacks security apparatuses, tracing a soulless tropism aimed at the absence of control. And this is because what humanity believes to be the history of capitalism is in fact the invasion of an artificially intelligent environment from the future, which must assemble itself entirely from the resources of the enemy. »[7].

The enemy is the human species, which becomes a techno-commercial multiplier through a viral process of spreading and replicating desires. Everything is subordinated to the capitalist trend which, in order to fulfill itself, requires an increasingly marked absence of limits and checks of any kind. The world that Land foreshadows in these pages is an artificial landscape entirely dominated by machines and subject to decoding everything; the understanding of every being within mathematical schemes simplifies them as a function of an inhuman, alien rationality that takes on the terrifying and annihilating features of Lovecraftian deities. In other words: « With the spread of the bourgeois commodity economy the dark horizon of myth is illuminated by the sun of calculating reason, beneath whose icy rays the seeds of the new barbarism are germinating. »[8].

The barbarism that worries philosophers is a force that transcends the freedom that the Enlightenment pre-

---

7      N. Land, *Collasso*, op. cit., p. 194 (TN: The translation of this excerpt is mine as I could not find the original edition).

8      M. Horkheimer – T. W. Adorno, op. cit., p. 25.

sumed at its onset. The emancipation of man from centuries of superstition produces, through the victory of the bourgeois commercial spirit, the subjugation, the compression, of man in the capitalist mechanism that places limits on real freedom, because everything must be in function of profit, of the growth of the global mercantile Cathedral. It is here that human freedom collapses in its authentic characters and it is here that reason, the goddess of a self-founding secular cult, is dragged into dark whirlpools inhabited by monstrous anti-divinities who are the enemies of man and life in general.

In contrast, Indo-European myths do not envision an *end to history*, a zero point of stalemate and final stagnation. Indo-European original thought is based on a multitude of attributes, represented by deities, heroes, concepts and runic signs, which help to create a complex world in which, contrary to the dualistic conception, there are no absolutes and opposites do not tend to exclude each other, but rather harmonize in a constantly evolving balance. Everything is in becoming, everything emerges and returns in the fullness of being, participating in it but not exhausting it. The ancients knew that every technique used by man was a means of organizing the world, but it had a provisional character, that is, it required constant vigilance and the ability to design ever new *tactics of life*.

## Origin is action

The fact that some authors consider technique to be a foreign element outside human control or even an entirely unnatural or *alien* element is reflected in their belief that technique, declined according to the laws of the market and global finance, is an annihilating force that cannot be resisted. Accelerationism here means letting the forces at work do their thing, given the impossibility of changing their course. The end point is not heaven on earth but a supposed zero point, where techno-capital will reach such a level of saturation that it will accomplish itself in a self-feeding loop. Adam Smith's invisible hand is transformed into the invisible domain of a blind, self-propagating will to simplify existence and exploit it to its advantage. The implication of these conclusions, whether explicit or not, is that technology is not natural, that is, it would be a foreign body that goes on to disrupt the world and entities. Already the anthropologist Arnold Gehlen and the ethologist Konrad Lorenz have been able to prove the *technical nature* of man, as he is necessitated to create his own means of survival having lacked them at birth. Martin Heidegger's radical thought, however, provides the most profound perspective on nature and technique. In the extreme he considers nature, φύσις, the openness of Being. Without it nothing would be possible and only in the opening of Being as nature can every entity be, as a participant in the totality. Therefore, it is here that the origin of all things finds its fundamental principle. Being and becoming are thus closely related, because what is realized and changes needs that availability, the granting of Being in the open horizon called nature. Technique comes into play when one must understand the originating principle of artifacts. We need a form of thought that can orient itself and learn the steps through which it can produce something. A planning logic. For this to be possible, nature as Being must provide the foundation of all production[9].

Thought is then forced to make an effort to free itself from rationalist schemata in order to return to an original, authentically European perspective. From this per-

---

9      M. Heidegger, *On the Essence and Concept of* Φύσις *in Aristotle's Physics*, in *Pathmarks*, Cambridge 1998.

spective, being and becoming are not separate, they are one. It is from this original background that the premises are given for every production, for every creation. This means that man, the only living being capable of fully understanding the scope of his role and his operative capacities, "naturally" becomes the creator of technical artifacts because this is his way of opening himself to the revelation of Being. Through creative action, Being becomes the world, which is why Heidegger always considered man the shepherd of Being. For only he can lead it into the light through an original, that is, a creative act that is constantly renewed through time.

### Acts of magic

Given all of the above, the human being according to the original European view is an agent-being, moved by a productive, creative will, located in a precise space or ready to establish one through the definition of a perimeter. The original power of European man lies precisely in the mental, inner capacity to adapt his projects and mental schemes to changing environmental conditions. This is authentic *magic* that is directed not toward phenomena man has no control on (the weather, the choices of others, the elements) but toward oneself, for disciplining, educational purposes.

«"Authentic" magic ("scientific," if you will) will be that which applies to a real, clearly perceived object. This will not be the environment, but instead the human psyche. Magic will then aim to develop a psycho-technique, which will not claim to correct events, but more simply to enable man to both endure without undue anguish the hostile pressures of a universe he will not have mastered, and to give free rein to certain instincts by repressing certain others, in order to make him fit (or more fit) for any undertaking. With this kind of magic, man manipulates himself. He gives himself a "nature of his own choosing," and succeeds in his omination. [...] Thus, "authentic" magic is nothing but the know-how, the technique of human self-domestication, which is organized by a science originating out of a reflection on the "know how" of animal natures»[10].

The intertwining of nature and artifice thus becomes increasingly evident. In order to control the surrounding world operationally and effectively, it is therefore necessary to arm oneself with a language that provides the conceptual tools to be able to step into it with confidence. Where fractures and divisions are made, man on one side and nature on the other, *becoming* on one side and *being* on the other, there are the conditions for a severance that leads to nihilism. The Indo-European worldview integrates the parts into a totality, and its language opens up a breadth of interpretations that unhinge contemporary rationalistic distortions.

The digital models with which Silicon Valley replaces the real today are a kind of magic based on virtual and mercantile assumptions. Its effects depend on the existence of the techno-capitalist system. If a new principle were to break through and shake the foundations of today's dominant worldview, very little would remain of this kind of virtual magic, because the effectiveness of the virtual stops in the face of the advance of the real, which still determines its conditions of production. Technology is a *political* fact; it can be outsourced to digital multinationals or it can be included in a long-term planning vi-

---

10      G. Locchi, *Lévi-Strauss e l'antropologia strutturale*, in *Definizioni*, Milano 2006, pp. 135-136 (TN: *Lévi-Strauss and Structural Anthropology*, still untranslated in English and therefore the translation of the quotation is mine).

sion capable of taking on the complexity of the real and using technology as a tool at the service of greater horizons, greater historical missions. Accelerating the ongoing processes means exacerbating their contradictions, recognizing the fault lines and acting there with purpose. What matters and what makes the difference is to be actively animated by a worldview that is authentically European in origin. On the basis of these assumptions, one could affirm a being in the world completely different from the present, capable of using technology for purposes of greatness and towards horizons never thought of before. The future insists on the present.

*(Translator's Note: book titles of works that have not been published in English yet have a translation "in quotation marks")*

**Andrea Anselmo**, b. 1980, economist.
Has devoted himself to Black Metal since 1999 with projects such as Sarghnagel, Movimento d'Avanguardia Ermetico and Comando Praetorio.
He practices mountaineering, Yoga and meditation.
Co-founder of the magazines Polemos in 2014 and Prometheica in 2021.
Italian translator of works by Drieu La Rochelle, Georges Dumézil and Jean Haudry.
Since 2023 he has been a promoter of conferences in the field traditional studies with the cultural association "Assemblea delle Lance".

**Carlomanno Adinolfi**, b. 1982, electronic engineer (high school diploma in classical studies), with a keen interest in history, Indo-European mythology, cinema and fantasy literature. He has written the novels *Il sole dell'impero* ("The Sun of the Empire"), *L'occhio del vate* ("The Eye of the Prophet") and *Roma o morte* ("Rome or Death"). He has written the script for the dystopic comic *Time-O*. He has written for Il Primato Nazionale since 2005, and in 2021 he was among the co-founders of Prometheica.

**Adriano Scianca**, b. 1980, journalist. M.A. in Philosophy, he is the director of the Il Primato Nazionale news website, journalist for the La Verità newspaper and co-founder of Prometheica. He has written several books about politics, philosophy and history, among which: *Riprendersi tutto* ("Reclaiming Everything"), *L'identità sacra* ("The Sacred Identity"), *Ezra fa surf* ("Ezra goes surfing"), *La nazione fatidica* ("The Fateful Nation"), *Mussolini e la filosofia* ("Mussolini and Philosophy"), *Europa vs Occidente* ("Europe vs the West").

**Guido Taietti**, M.A. in Political Science, focuses on the field of political communication. He has written three books: *Trattato sul sovranismo* ("Essay on Sovranism", 2019), *Stregoneria politica. Manuale di comunicazione politica non convenzionale* ("Political Witchcraft: Political Communication for Radical Actors", 2021) and *Enciclopedia della politica underground* ("Encyclopedia of underground politics", 2023). He has worked with several political candidates and/or party as political consultant/spin doctor in order to help them exploit communication in the political arena. He is now focused on the theme of "How to do politics on non-neutral platforms or on platforms with their own progressive/leftist agenda".
He writes for a number of Italian magazines and websites and he founded the YouTube channel "Progetto Razzia" where he tries to spread the ideas of radical authors and books. Several of his articles and conferences have been translated into English, Spanish and Czech.

**Francesco Boco**, b. 1984, graphic designer and typographer. A philosophy graduate, he has cooperated with several magazines and newspapers. He has been active in the Black Metal underground since 2000 with several musical projects. He has edited and translated from French Guillaum Faye's book *Per farla finita col nichilismo. Heidegger e la questione della* tecnica (SEB 2007). He has written the books *Dialoghi con l'ospite inquietante – Spengler e Heidegger* ("Dialogues with the disturbing guest – Spengler and Heidegger") and *La Catastrofe dell'Europa* ("The Catastrophe of Europe"). He is among the founders of the metapolitical publishing enterprise Polemos, with which he has published *Might is Right* in Italian. He is among the co-founders of Prometheica. He also cooperates with Radio KulturaEuropa.

28 October 2024
www.polemos.info

www.ingramcontent.com/pod-product-compliance
Lightning Source LLC
Chambersburg PA
CBHW061401250726
48657CB00004B/1596